A Journey Towards Poetry

JOHN MOGAN

Order this book online at www.trafford.com
or email orders@trafford.com

Most Trafford titles are also available at major online book retailers.

Printed in the United States of America.

ISBN: 978-1-4669-2051-4 (sc)
ISBN: 978-1-4669-2285-3 (e)

Library of Congress Control Number: 2012906057

Trafford rev. 04/20/2012

 www.trafford.com

North America & international
toll-free: 1 888 232 4444 (USA & Canada)
phone: 250 383 6864 ♦ fax: 812 355 4082

DEDICATION

This book is dedicated to
Donald Smith
a high school teacher who taught me
the color and the harmony
in the music of poetry
and to my older brother
Donley Mogan
whose insights into music and literature
have astounded me all my life.

TABLE OF CONTENTS

PROLOGUE

My Journey Towards Poetry

A journey towards poetry is, of course, my journey towards poetry. Looking backward, I can see that my entire life has been that journey. Not a trip! A trip is there and back again; with a journey, there's no going back. There may be side-trips, and maybe trip-ups, but a journey moves on. Towards a goal? Hopefully. An attainable one? Perhaps. A knowable one? Only in part, for though many have started the journey, I have never heard of anyone who arrived at journey's end. So what and where is journey's end? Poetry!

I have felt a music and a magic in poetry since as far back as I can remember. From a time before I could read, there was a thrill in the sound of these opening lines:

> By Nebo's lonely mountain,
> On this side Jordan's wave,
> In a vale in the land of Moab,
> There lies a lonely grave;
> And no man knows that sepulchre,
> And no man saw it e'er,

For the angels of God upturned the sod
And laid the dead man there.
  Cecil Frances Alexander (1818-1895) *The Burial of Moses*

The strange names in the first three lines with the change in rhythm and mysterious action in the last two line were like an enchantment to me. Another enchantment was this half-forgotten poem called <u>The Witching Pool</u> *from an early school grade reader:*

Down in the fern-brake, dim and cool,
Drowning the stars, lies the witching pool…
…Soft - stay - tall reeds sway,
Ripples rise and drift away,
Lilies lift - petals fall,
Swift come the notes of the magic call…
There, every night, in their silver shoon
The woodfolk dance to a magic tune.

The pauses and rests, like the pauses and rests in musical notation, created verbal music.

At the University of Toronto, I studied English Language and Literature. Undergraduate courses failed to explain the music and magic that enchanted me, so I applied to the Graduate School for my Masters in English while I taught English in high school. Graduate school didn't explain the music and magic any better.

I left teaching and went into medicine. After six years of family practice, I accepted a fellowship in psychiatry at Harvard University. Psychiatry bound together everything I had studied before. With its focus on feelings and the verbalization of emotion, it opened to me the world of the non-

rational and directed my quest for poetry in new directions. So the journey towards poetry continues still. My journey has two limits: its scope is the language I speak—English; its duration is the rest of my life.

1

Efforts to Define Poetry

In Western Europe, books and writings stretch from Homeric times to the age of the printing press, while writings from the Middle East and Egypt survive from ages before Homer. Those writings contain many poems, but almost no attempts to define poetry or to explain the making of poems. In all this body of writing one work on poetry exists dating from Roman times. That is the _Ars Poetica_ by the poet Horace (65-8 bce). For him, making poetry was a mixture of _ars_ and _ingenium_, translated as _inspiration_ and _craftsmanship_. Literary critics have agreed on the words but disagreed about their meaning.

Definitions of poetry in English started to appear in the 16th century. An early work was _An Apology for Poetry_ by Sir Philip Sidney (1554-1586). Justifying the English language as appropriate for the writing of poetry, he contended that poetry should educate and lead a reader toward virtue. This primary educative function of poetry lasted until the 18th century.

The 17th and 18th centuries had great poets, but little definition of poetry. In his _Essay on Criticism_, Alexander Pope (1688-

1744) spoke as an evaluator and critic, presenting examples of poetic technique, but no definition or explication:

> True ease in writing comes from art, not chance,
> As those move easiest who have learn'd to dance.
> 'Tis not enough no harshness gives offence,
> The sound must seem an echo to the sense.

Each line from this point illustrates through example how the sound must be an echo to the sense of what is said.

> Soft is the strain when Zephyr gently blows,
> And the smooth stream in smoother numbers flows;
> But when loud surges lash the sounding shore,
> The hoarse, rough verse should like the torrent roar.
> When Ajax strives some rock's vast weight to throw,
> The line too labours, and the words move slow;
> Not so, when swift Camilla scours the plain,
> Flies o'er th' unbending corn, and skims along the main.
> Hear how Timotheus' varied lays surprise,
> And bid alternate passions fall and rise!
>
> Essay on Criticism II ll.362-375

With the arrival of romanticism in the late 18th century, the educative purpose of poetry waned. In the _Lyrical Ballads_ (1898) by Wordsworth and Coleridge, Wordsworth (1770-1850) wrote in the _Introduction_:

> _"All good poetry is the spontaneous overflow of powerful feelings"._

Later in that *Introduction* he returned to his definition:

> *"I have said that poetry is the spontaneous overflow of powerful feelings: it takes its origin from emotion recollected in tranquility. The emotion is contemplated till, by a species of reaction, the tranquility gradually disappears, and an emotion, kindred to that which was before the subject of contemplation, is gradually produced, and does itself actually exist in the mind. In this mood successful composition generally begins, and in a mood similar to this it is carried on; but the emotion, of whatever kind, and in whatever degree, from various causes, is qualified by various pleasure, so that in describing any passions whatsoever, which are voluntarily described, the mind will, upon the whole, be in a state of enjoyment."*

There is no way to understand his phrases "by a species of reaction" and "various pleasures". Both definition and explanation seem to be personal and apply specifically to Wordsworth's own poetic process. In the last stanza of his poem *I Wandered Lonely as a Cloud* he exemplifies that process:

> For oft when on my couch I lie
> In vacant or in pensive mood,
> They[1] flash upon that inner eye   [1] (*daffodils*)
> Which is the bliss of solitude;
> And then my heart with pleasure fills,
> And dances with the daffodils.

In addition, it is difficult to reconcile Wordsworth's definition of poetry taking its origin from emotion recollected in tranquility with the excitement of Byron's *Destruction of Senacherib* or the restless violence of Browning's *Pied Piper of Hamelin*.

Shelley (1792-1822), in his _Defence of Poetry_, said:

> "_Poetry is not, like reasoning, a power to be exerted according to the determination of the will. A man cannot say, 'I will compose poetry.' The greatest poet even cannot say it; for the mind in creation is as a fading coal, which some invisible influence, like an inconstant wind, awakens to transitory brightness; this power arises from within, like the color of a flower which fades and changes as it is developed, and the conscious portions of our nature are unprophetic either of its approach or its departure._"

That is very beautiful, and conveys an awe connected with the process of creation which the poet who creates it does not understand, but it does not define poetry; it gives a metaphor for the creative process itself.

Laurence Perrine (1915-1995) in _Sound and Sense_, says:

> "_Poetry might be defined as a kind of language that says more and says it more intensely than does ordinary language._"

The definition is good, but it leaves problems unresolved. How does that _language_ (whatever the kind) say whatever _it_ is more intensely? Wherein does _intensely_ lie? In addition there is no reference to music or to musical effects in language.

Burton Raffel (1928-), himself a great poet and translator, in _How to Read a Poem_, wrote:

> "_Poetry is a disciplined compact verbal utterance in some more or less musical mode dealing with aspects of internal or external reality in some meaningful way._"

This, again, is a good definition. It acknowledges *musical mode* as essential to poetry, but requires more explanation and expansion for these terms: *(a) disciplined, (b) aspects of internal or external reality,* and *(c) meaningful way.*

Harold Bloom (1930-) in *The Best Poems of the English Language from Chaucer through Robert Frost*, says:

> *"Poetry is in the first place a high and ancient art. It raises your consciousness of glory and of grief, of woe or wonder as Shakespeare phrased it. Poetry essentially is figurative language concentrated so that its form is both expressive and evocative. Figuration is a departure from the literal."*

This is an excellent definition. The phrase "*high and ancient art*" suggests and implies great practice with language and a knowledge of tradition before a writer can assume the title *poet*. Through the words *glory, grief, woe,* and *wonder,* he stresses the importance of an emotional dimension if the work is to be called poetry. For three words and phrases, however, more explanation is needed – (a) *consciousness*, (b) *figurative language* and (c) *evocative*. In addition, the definition lacks reference to the music or musicality of language.

Children's definitions, e.g. *A poem is a rainbow in words*, are imaginative pseudo-definitions. Poetic attempts like *"A gesture in space and lo! there's the triolet"* fail because they use a metaphor which neither defines nor explains anything.

There is another one cited frequently: "*Poetry is condensed prose.*" If so, then the converse has to be true: "Prose is diffuse poetry". Prose may be many things, but it is not diffuse poetry.

In the dictionaries, there is little or no help. The *Oxford English Dictionary* assumes an opposition between poetry and prose, and explains neither one well. The *Merriam Webster*

Dictionary, has many definitions for poetry, but one stands out unlike any other encountered:

> "*writing that formulates a concentrated imaginative awareness of experience in language chosen and arranged to create a specific emotional response through the meaning, sound, and rhythm.*"

That is a definition requiring serious thought. It stresses *emotional response*, but it lacks any direct reference to music, though it approaches some of the attributes of music when it mentions *sound* and *rhythm*.

Through all of these attempts to explain poetry, little attention is paid to the relationship between music and poetry. Since poetry is created through language and verbal sound, the relationship of poetry to sound and music must be examined.

2

Language

If a man runs into a meeting room with his mouth open, arms raised, and eyes staring about, someone might say, "You look frightened to death." If he says, "I am," silent questions boil in the air of the room. But if he answers, "When I got out of my car, somebody with a knife at the edge of the parking lot shouted and ran toward me, so I bolted in here," then not only has he explained his appearance, but each listener has participated in the terror he felt.

Those two responses illustrate the simplest and clear-cut levels in two uses of language. The first answer, "I am", is conversation-stopping agreement: someone says he looks a certain way; he affirms it. The second and longer answer is a word picture explaining his appearance and his listeners share not only his situation but also his response to the experience. The first response conveys fact; the second response creates emotional experience.

Language is one of the most complex, elaborate, and awe-inspiring creations of humankind, growing, shifting, and changing in an organic way. It is multifarious in shape, multi-tonal in form, with hundreds and thousands of articulations in range and dialect. In their growth since being invented in the 18th century, dictionaries illustrate how language has altered and evolved like a living creature.

Noam Chomsky (1928-) proposes that language is an instinct, and that there is a part of the human brain created and adapted like a grid on which language is laid. If it is true, that fact only testifies to the importance of language for humans. It performs a myriad of functions: among other things, it allows humans to think, to communicate, to reason abstractly, to create new ideas, to organize factual material, and to communicate emotions. In that last function, it is helped by tone of voice, and all the devices of speech that are called "poetic" and "musical".

Language plays with itself in simple spoonerisms – *palt and sepper* (salt and pepper) – and in more complex ones – *e-toastric lecter* (electric toaster). It plays with itself in pseudo-languages like Pig-Latin – *ead-ray is-thay* (read this) – and Obish – *dobance boball-ober-obin-oba* (dance ballerina). Language is used for play in word-games like riddles and puns, and since pre-history, it has carried magical power through charms, enchantments, and incantations (singings). It may be used also for the casting of spells by voice and through runic writing

The joy and delight in language, with the fun arising from its twists and distortions demonstrate its human origin. It is a shifting developing creation that fascinates and entrances. It shapes reasoning and cognition, and can carry emotional messages that develop parallel to its content. Some of the emotional burden lies more in the tone of voice than in the meaning of the words.

People writing about the development of language in children, remark on how they start with sounds expressive of emotion, develop to words denoting people and things, and then pass through words dealing with space (where) and time (when) into areas of abstract meaning (the qualities of things). the process of formation (how) and the cause (why).

No language, however, contains many words for feelings or emotions. There are some *names* for emotions, but the conveying of emotion itself depends on tone of voice, facial expression, body language, or narrative example.

If we turn to music, the slow movement in musical compositions expresses introspective emotions like sadness, or some other gentle mood. There are hundreds and thousands of slow movements each expressing different shades of emotion, but there aren't enough words in any dictionary to begin expressing the exact emotion in all those slow symphonic movements.

Can language express feelings and emotions? Maybe. Here is the word *fear* defined in the Merriam Webster Dictionary:

1. *(a) an unpleasant emotional state characterized by anticipation of pain or great distress and accompanied by heightened autonomic activity especially involving the nervous system: agitated foreboding often of some real or specific peril (compare anxiety)*
   (b) an Instance or manifestation of this feeling
   (c) calm recognition or consideration of whatever may injure or damage; reasoned caution; intelligent foresight.
2. *(a) the state or habit of feeling agitation or dismay; a condition between anxiety and terror either natural and well-grounded or unreasoned and blind.*
   (b) anxious concern; solicitude
3. *profound reverence and awe*

> *4. something that is the object of apprehension or alarm;*
> *a ground for fear*

That definition has lots of synonyms and names of other emotions, but a reader comes away knowing that the lexicographer has only substituted one word for another. This definition is fear as *fact*, not fear as *experience*. That distinction harks back to the anecdote which started this section, presenting fact in the first example and participatory experience in the second.

Language has two elements: meaning, and emotional impact. Meaning pervades all language, and can exist alone. Sometimes, however, in addition to meaning, language can create an emotional impact, and this impact is called "poetic". The power to move a reader or hearer emotionally confers on language poetical or "magical" properties. These functions of language will be repeated many times in this writing.

Poetry's magic is like any magic – the magic of spells where statement or writing holds power over objects or people, or the magic of enchantment whose meaning comes from the word "chant" or "sing" having the same power. For Harry Potter, spells are in Latin-like words. In most stories where a spell is written, sounds with no meaning are used. Every language has musical sounds without meaning from tra-la-la, toora-loora-loora, and tiddly-um-dum-dum to scat singing with Ella Fitzgerald and Cleo Laine.

The magic and music of poetry depend upon the basic elements of language itself. These elements are sounds which are not necessarily the letters we read (icons). The alphabet of any written language attempts to catch, in a spatial icon, the sounds used in speaking the language. They never succeed well because there are more gradations of sound than there are letters in any alphabet. There is an international phonetic alphabet, but no one writes in it. So instead of starting with a classification of the letters of the alphabet, the classification here is going to start with the sounds themselves, and the way the mouth makes them.

3

The Elements of Language

Spoken language is a flow of vowel sounds interrupted by consonants. Starting with consonants, an attempt will be made to move sounds spatially from the front of the mouth to the back, so that the sounds will have the quality of coming at first from the lips, then moving back through the space between the teeth and lips to the teeth, followed by the tongue and palate, and finally to the sounds from the throat.

h - e   The first consonantal sounds will be only the spirated or breathed sounds, voiced and unvoiced, represented in English by the letter "h" in "have" or "hip", and the schwa or "e" as in "the". The first is a voiceless sound – only a breath; the second is a grunt.

wh (hw) - w   The second group of sounds is a pair. They are produced by blowing air through the lips. The first sound is "wh" as in "where" and "what". The second sound is produced by using the voice as you blow air through the lips and that is "w" as in "were" and "watt". Anglo-Saxon spelled the first sound "hw" to indicate how they heard it.

p - m - b   The next group, three in number, are formed by using only the lips with or without the voice. The voiceless sound from the lips is "p" as in "pea" or "poor". The voiced sound is made in exactly the same way, using the lips, but with the voice to produce "b" as in "bee" or "boor". These two are explosive – they can't be sustained. The third one adds resonance from the nasal sinuses with vibration of the lips, "m", as in "me" or "moor". What is the connection is between m, p, and b? The way you make the sounds. If you say "me-me" and then hold the nose closed, you will hear "be-be"; all three sounds are made from the lips alone and you can test this by saying the three sounds to yourself a few times. You will find that the lips move slightly away from the teeth as you say the sounds.

f - v   The fourth group is also a pair. They are made with the upper teeth against the lower lip to produce friction in the air flow producing the voiceless "f" as in "fine" and the voiced "v" as in "vine".

th - th (eth)   The fifth group is peculiarly English: they are the sounds made by setting the tongue against the upper teeth and blowing out the breath to produce the unvoiced "th" as in "thing" or the voiced "th" as in "there". Anglo-Saxon distinguished between these with letters called the "thorn" (unvoiced) and the "eth" (voiced).

t - n - d   The sixth group of three sounds are "dentals" produced by the tongue against the back of the teeth: the voiceless "t" as in "toe", the voiced "d" as in "doe", and nasal-dental sound "n" as in "no". The "t" and "d" again are non-sustainable. Once again you can find the connection between "d" and "n" by saying "no" and holding your nose. What you hear is "doe". These sounds come from the teeth: "t" is voiceless, "d" is voiced, and "n" is nasal.

s - z   Next come the hissing sounds or sibilants. The first pair are made with the teeth held together, the tongue against the lower teeth, and the lips stretched wide. These two sounds are the unvoiced "s" as in "ass" and voiced "s" as in "as". Often the voiced "s" is spelled "z" as in "zoo" to contrast with the unvoiced "s" in "sue". Sibilants can be lengthened or sustained.

sh - zh   The second pair of sibilants occur as the unvoiced "sh" as in "assure" and the companion voiced sound as in "azure". To make them, the teeth are held together, the tongue back, and the lips rounded. Once again, these sounds can be sustained over time.

ch - j   The third pair of sibilant consonantal sounds is the unvoiced "ch" as in "cheer" and the voiced form usually written "j" as in "jeer". These are formed in a way similar to "sh" and "ch", but they are short explosive sounds and can't be sustained.

k - ng - g   The next consonants are the glottals made from the back of the mouth: the unvoiced is "k" or hard "c"; the voiced is "g" and the nasal is "ng".

The first can be heard in "back"; the voiced form in "bag" and the nasal in "bang". If you hold your nose, the word "bang" becomes "bag". Among these sounds "k" and "g" are non-sustainable.

kh - gh   The last group of consonants is complex – the gutturals with various spellings. The first is the unvoiced "kh" as in the German "ach" and the second is the voiced guttural in the gargling noise "gh". English has kept none of the gutturals. They come from Anglo-Saxon words like "rough" and "night", and persist in Scottish dialectal language. Sustainable? No.

It is noticeable that the move from the sibilants (s – z – s – zh – ch – j) to the glottals (k – ng – g) is a leap from the front of the mouth to the back. What sounds are made in between? They are the letters "l" and "r". They are called "liquids" and are made in a variety of ways. They sit not only between the front of the mouth and the back, but they also sit halfway between the consonants which interrupt the flow of vowel sound, and the vowel sounds themselves. They are called "liquids" because they can be sung, unlike most of the other consonants.

l - r   The "l" sound can be positioned at the front of the mouth, at the palate medially, and at the glottis at the back of the mouth. The same is true for the "r" sound which, in addition to placement, can be trilled either at the front of the mouth, or at the back with the uvular "r" of good French pronunciation.

? ? ? ?   A final group of sounds has no icons, but can be described: they are called "clicks". The four of them involve inhaling or breathing air in rather than breathing out as the previous sounds demand. In this physical way they differ from all the other sounds. To classify, they will be described as sounds produced moving from the front of the mouth to the back. The first starts with the lips pursed together followed by the sucking sound of kissing. The second is the disapproving sound produced by inhaling the voiceless "th" with the lips separated and the tongue placed just behind the upper teeth with a quick sucking sound; this is often written "tsk tsk". The third is the click with the tongue on the upper palate and a quick suction as the tongue is pulled away from the palate – it sounds like the cork coming out of a bottle. Fourth is a pair of voiced and unvoiced sucking sound at the glottis itself – the unvoiced sounds like a choke, while the voiced sounds like a frog croaking. Some languages from Africa use the first two clicks; the last two are used in some native American languages.

Here is a classification of English consonant sounds as a table:

	Unvoiced	Nasal	Voiced	
spirates	h		uh*	
spirate-labials	wh		w	The asterisks
labials	p	m**	b	indicate voiced
fricatives	f		v*	consonant sounds
dento-linguals	th		th*	which can be
dentals	t	n**	d	sustained on a
sibilants #1	s		z*	musical tone with

sibilants #2	sh		zh*	only slight inter-
sibilants #3	ch		j	ference. Nasals-
glottals	k	ng**	g	and liquids can be
gutturals	ch(ach)		gh	sung, and are very
lingual-liquids			l & r***	close to vowels.
clicks (no icons)				

Among the consonant sounds, only the voiced ones can sound a musical note briefly, and only the nasals and liquids can sustain a note; the unvoiced ones cannot be sung. Try this to prove to yourself the truth of that claim.

The next sound-group is the vowels. They can be described as voiced sounds involving the use of the vocal cords and occur spatially as the sound is shaped and moved from the front of the mouth back across the top of the palate to the throat, and then come forward across the tongue and the floor of the mouth to return in a circle, as it were, to the front of the mouth.

peel -- pale -- pal -- pall -- pole -- pool -- pull --
putt -- pot --par -- pat -- pet -- pell -- pill -- peel

And there are sounds outside that neat circle, and sounds which combine elements of the circle. First is the yod as in "you"; second is the schwa as in the. Then there are diphthongs moving from the front of the mouth to the back:

bay -- buy -- boy -- bough

There is a tradition going back to the writing of the Bible and to the ancient Greeks that the name of god is pure vowel. The traditional pronunciation of "Jahweh" can be transcribed as **yaw-way**. The production of that is by a rapid movement through the circle of vowel sounds from the lips, across the palate or roof of the mouth to the glottis, and back across the floor of the tongue and mouth to the lips. If you say it very slowly, you can feel the sound move as described. Vowels as sounded breath have an ancient association with holiness. But those things need not concern the presentation here of the sounds of language first through consonants and then through vowels.

When, along with sound, sense is added, then traditions in the use of language become relevant to consideration.

In spoken language, there can be sound without sense. Clearly sounds precede both words and sense. What sounds do this? Basically vowel sounds. As was said earlier, language can be defined as a stream of vowel sound interrupted and punctuated by consonant which, generally, arrest or break the flow. The word "generally" is placed there because liquids sounds (l, r), the nasals (m, n, ng), and the other voiced consonants (v, th, z, zh) can partially carry the stream of vocalic sound also.

"So what?" may be a legitimate question. This material sounds far removed from the world of practicality and the world of poetry. Perhaps! But there are three kinds of people who are interested in the two extremes, at one end the constantly interrupting consonants, and at the other end the flow of vowel sound.

Almost all students are interested in the first – the consonant pattern. This is the basis of texting and speed-writing, and those who take notes learn quickly to eliminate the vowels, because the consonants by themselves will produce quite accurately the sense of what a person has said. Here is an example—hr s n xmpl. When the focus is on sense, there is little time for vowel music.

Singers, on the other hand, focus on the vowels and the few consonant groups mentioned above that will sustain a musical note. What they would like to do is eliminate all other consonants because they interrupt the musical flow. Anyone who has sung in a glee club or choir will understand immediately why this desire is justified.

What does a singer hear in language? Here are the important things in decreasing order of importance:

(a) The first order of sounds will be the long vowels sounds as in words like the following: w**ee**, w**ay**, **eye**, **awe**, w**oe**, w**oo**.

(b) The second order of sounds will be the short vowels as in words like the following: w**e**ll, w**a**re, w**a**n, w**o**re, l**u**re, r**u**m, r**i**m.

(c) The third order of sounds will be the voiced consonants that can be sustained. These were mentioned before: the liquids -l- as in "all" and -r- as in "far", the nasals -m- as in "calm" -n- as in "cannon" and -ng- as in "sing", and the mixed voiced group – -v- as in "mauve", -z- as in "haze", -zh- as in "azure", and -th- as in "the"

(d) The fourth order will be all the other voiced consonants as in **b**an, **w**on, **d**in, **g**one, **j**im.

(e) The last order will be all the unvoiced consonants as in **h**a**h**a, **p**e**p**, **wh**ee, **f**i**f**e, **t**a**t**, **th**in, **s**as**s**, **c**oc**k**, **sh**u**sh**, **ch**ur**ch**. Three of these – sss, shhh, and chhh – can be sustained, and are used to attract attention or to command silence

Singers hate all those last unvoiced sounds because they are unsingable.

Poets are the last group of people interested in these sounds. Spenser recorded his study in *The Shepherd's Calendar*, an exercise in verse patterns, sounds and rhythms. Milton recorded his study in the poems *L'Allegro* and *Il Penseroso* – the first an invocation to Mirth, and the second to Melancholy. Tennyson, boating with Fitzgerald (*Rubaiyat* man) said, "Fitz, I know the sound value of every words in English except, perhaps, scissors." These poets studied sound and practiced word and rhythm like exercises on a musical instrument.

These consonant and vowel sounds were called the "elements of language" in the title of the chapter. They are the raw material from which language is created and shaped. Then language clothes both thought and emotion.

In a chemical analogy, sounds are the elements which join together to form compounds – words. The words (compounds) are given meaning but their sounds may change over time according to the language laws of phonology and morphology.

4

Interlude: The Geography of Language

This journey towards poetry will move through a geographical landscape. Meaning, definition, and the whole array of facts with logic, mathematics and science, form a continental mass – the Continent of Sense. Around that Land of Sense lies the Sea of Sound – sometimes organized sound (music), and sometimes disorganized sound (noise).

This journey winds from the land where comprehension and meaning are important, across a beach to the shallows of the Sea of Sound, where sense becomes less important, and sound becomes more so. Poetry lives on that beach.

Like all journeys, it moves from landscapes that are known, and proceeds through less familiar vistas into unknown territory. It starts where knowledge of the language is necessary and must be understood, and passes into areas where meaning fades and sound begins to dominate sense. Before moving towards the Sea of Sound, it is important to explain what regions form the Continent of Sense – the land on which this journey is turning its back.

A central area of the Land of Sense is occupied by the Desert of Abstraction surrounding the Mountain of Mathematics with its unscalable Pi pinnacle. In the foothills are the minor ranges of Applied Physics, Applied Chemistry and applied Sciences, with the Mines of Engineering. Surrounding that mountain, on the Desert of Abstraction, lie the many oases of Philosophy and Logic.

Around the Desert of Abstraction lie the Rainforests of Words teeming with the rich vocabularies of every spoken tongue and all sensory perceptions. From the Rainforests outward to the coasts stretch lands cultivated with five crops. On the plains are the prairies of Exposition where language is cultivated to be logical in thought, unified in structure, precise in expression, and above all else, clear. In this area there are tiny groves containing the rhetorical devices that can be applied to the expression of reasonable language. In the river valleys and wetlands lie lush forests of Description. Here all five senses are cultivated with particular attention to the arrangement of materials into foreground, middleground, and background. In glens and dales along the rivers and waterways lie the colorful farmlands of Narrative. Each one is different from the next, with emphasis on plot, character, setting, and mood. Where land is poor, there are the factory-towns of Advocacy where language is used to sell, to convince, and to mislead. And finally where nothing else will grow there are Lists – directories and telephone books.

This journey turns its back on that Continent of Meaning, that Land of Sense, and winds across the beach where logic and language become confused with sound and with other characteristics that have been loosely called "poetic".

5

Poetry as Fact

A listener or reader can say what a poem is about, figure out who the speaker is, state the viewpoint, and determine whether or not the viewpoint is consistent. To apprehend *content* and to formulate *meaning* for a poem, you have to understand the language. Even such a lyric as this famous quatrain from William Blake's <u>*Auguries of Innocence*</u> presents facts and has meaning:

> To see a world in a grain of sand,
> And a heaven in a wild flower;
> Hold infinity in the palm of your hand,
> And eternity in an hour.

So poetry is rooted in the Land of Sense and has meaning.

For centuries those things called poems had a form that distinguished them from other writing. Traditional poetry seemed to be preoccupied with form as if, somehow, form created poetry. When a poet sat down to write a poem, he expressed himself within the parameters of a form with meter and rhyme scheme. The most zealous sticklers for form, however, could still accept "prose poetry" whose tradition went back at least as far as Baudelaire with his _Petits Poèmes en Prose_ published in 1869.

The last sentence of _The Masque of the Red Death_ by Poe (1809-1849) can be seen and experienced as poetry. Here it is re-aligned:

> And now was acknowledged the presence
> of the Red Death.
> He had come like a thief in the night.
> And one by one dropped the revellers
> in the blood-bedewed halls of their revel,
> and died each in the despairing posture of his fall.
> And the life of the ebony clock went out
> with that of the last of the gay.
> And the flames of the tripods expired.
> And Darkness and Decay and the Red Death
> held illimitable dominion over all.

That passage evokes an emotional response beyond what the words say similar to what is often experienced in poetry. Clearly _form_ need not be part of a solution to an understanding of poetry.

In 1950, during a class in Modern Poetry with Marshall McLuhan, some argument arose about the nature of poetry, and he said, "Don't ask what poetry _is_; ask what poetry _does_." So there are two basic questions about poetry that require answers: (a) what does poetry do? and (b) how does poetry work?

Help for answers to those questions came to me from many sources like the poets and scholars mentioned above – Horace, Wordsworth, Shelley, Perrine, Raffel, and Bloom. Unusual insights came from *The White Goddess, a Grammar of Poetic Myth* by Robert Graves (1895-1985).

But before taking up the questions what poetry does and how poetry works, I must take another look at the functions of language.

As was said before, language has two principal uses, and these uses can be connected to the great split in each individual between the facts of life – the incidents like pieces of a jigsaw puzzle that make up a life – and the emotional reactions the person experiences to those facts. That split exists in actuality if the functions of the left brain and the right brain are compared and contrasted. These are not precisely exact, but close enough to truth so that we can work with them.

Since the 19th century, neurologists have tried to identify areas of the brain where functions reside. Sensory and motor function are parallel on both sides of the brain. Some functions, though, are one-sided. 19th century neurologists working among the coal miners of Wales found that damage to the left brain destroyed the words to a song, but left the melody intact. In a similar way, damage to the right brain destroyed the melody of a song though the miner could still say the words. From that time up to the present, functions have been mapped and located in specific areas of the brain.

Language, logic, and mathematics reside in the dominant hemisphere of the brain (the left brain in right-handed people), and music with rhythm, melody, harmony, and mood – lie in the non-dominant hemisphere of the brain (the right brain in right-handed people), along with imagination and creativity.

In a mythological analogy, Athena, goddess of reason, rules the dominant hemisphere (logic, language, and mathematics). The nine Muses rule the non-dominant hemisphere (inspiration, imagination, music, and creativity).

Form cannot dictate whether a piece of writing is poetry or prose. Most people reading legal documents would say that they are dry and prosaic. Speeches like *The Gettysburg Address* and Lincoln's 2nd *Inaugural Address* are full of emotion, and have been described as passionate and poetic. These examples condense two uses of language mentioned before. One use is to communicate facts; the other is to create emotional experiences. "Two times two is four" is fact; "Yuk" and "Ouch" are emotional experience. Most written work is a combination of the two.

The *way* in which something is stated coupled with the *response* to that statement – those are the factors defining whether the matter is poetry or prose.

The next portion of this journey looks at the *ways* in which things are said or written.

6

Vocabulary

Many of the simpler effects of poetry are found in the words and language used by the poet. In the _Introduction to the Lyrical Ballads_ of 1798, mentioned before, Wordsworth (1770-1850) thought that the language of poetry should be the language of the common man, and he disliked the artificial classical vocabulary of authors like Pope who had preceded him:

> A little learning is a dangerous thing;
> Drink deep, or taste not the Pierian spring:
> There shallow draughts intoxicate the brain,
> And drinking largely sobers us again.
> Alexander Pope (1688-1744): *The Critic's Task*

Wordsworth, by contrast, wrote simply and movingly, and sits at the center of his poem. The final line allows a listener or reader to share his experience of loss.

She dwelt among the untrodden ways
    Beside the springs of Dove,
A Maid whom there were none to praise
    And very few to love:

A violet by a mossy stone
    Half hidden from the eye!
--Fair as a star, when only one
    Is shining in the sky.

She lived unknown, and few could know
    When Lucy ceased to be;
But she is in her grave, and, oh,
    The difference to me!
        William Wordsworth (1770-1850) *Lucy Poems*

By contrast, Wordsworth's fellow poet Coleridge used archaic language:

He holds him with his skinny hand,
    "There was a ship," quoth he.
"Hold off, unhand me, greybeard loon!"
    Eftsoons his hand dropped he.
    Coleridge (1772-1834) *The Rime of the Ancient Mariner*

The two poets, however, were not at odds. Wordsworth's simple lyric needed simple language; Coleridge's old ballad-story needed antique vocabulary.

Inversions of words like verbs and nouns, may help rhyme, rhythm, or musical effect, but they may sound artificial, as in this poem:

> Whither, midst falling dew,
> While glow the heavens with the last steps of day
> Far through their rosy depths dost thou pursue
> Thy solitary way?
> William Cullen Bryant (1794-1828): *To a Waterfowl*

Some poets distort language to achieve a local dialectal effect as with this Irish verse where English is used to reproduce the peculiarities of Erse:

> Mellow the moonlight to shine is beginning
> While close to the window young Eilleen is spinning
> *Irish song*

Some poets like Edith Sitwell contort language as she did in *Façade* to achieve a musical effect:

> Daisy and Lily,
> Lazy and silly,
> Walked by the shore of the wan grassy sea…..
> Edith Sitwell (1887-1964): *Façade – Waltz*

There are poets who make up language to write poetry, like *Jabberwocky* from *Alice Through the Looking-Glass*:

> 'Twas brillig, and the slithy toves
> Did gyre and gimble in the wabe.
> All mimsy were the borogoves,
> And the mome raths outgrabe.
> Lewis Carroll (1832-1898) *Alice Through the Looking Glass*

Words convey information on two levels. The first level is the denotative level – what the word means. The word *bully* could serve as an example. There is a dictionary definition. A second level is the emotional connotative level, and adds to the meaning in two ways. One is the level of knowledge shared by a people or a society. The noun *bully* has, beyond its denotation, a rich cloud of social connotation where people equate the word with stronger people abusing weaker ones. A second level of connotative meaning is personal – private to each hearer, and varies with individual experience. *Bully* evokes a denotative level and almost always both levels of connotation – social and personal.

The dullest prosaic fact may evoke profound personal connotative meaning arising from a person's experience. The odor of a pastry – a madeleine – dipped in tea summoned six volumes to Marcel Proust (1871-1922). For Emily Dickinson (1830-1886) words created ambience transporting readers through space and time.

> There is no frigate like a book
> To take us lands away,
> Nor any coursers like a page
> Of prancing poetry.
>
> This traverse may the poorest take
> Without oppress of toll;
> How frugal is the chariot
> That bears a human soul!

> Emily Dickinson (1830-1886)

So vocabulary affects the way a listener responds to what is written.

7

Structure

Just as there are musical dance forms like minuet, polonaise, and mazurka, so there are poetic forms like couplet, quatrain, ballad, sonnet and villanelle.

The forms in which poetry has been written are many, varied, and fascinating. It takes a technical knowledge of structure to compose a villanelle, and to balance the *octave* and the *sestet* of a sonnet. It requires taste to decide which subject matters lend themselves to Spenserean stanza, which ones to ballad meter, and which ones to blank verse or to prose poetry. And it takes inspiration to create a poem and shape it into one of these forms.

But as in music, where it is not the rhythm or form alone that makes the waltz, nor simply the rhythm or structure that makes a minuet, so in poetry it is not the form or structure that makes the poem. Hence, little time will be spent on structure except to present here part of a poem as paragraph and then in its original form.

That's my last Duchess painted on the wall, looking as if she were alive. I call that piece a wonder, now: Fra Pandolf's hands worked busily a day, and there she stands. Will 't please you sit and look at her? I said 'Fra Pandolf" by design, for never read strangers like you that pictured countenance, the depth and passion of its earnest glance, but to myself they turned…..

> That's my last Duchess painted on the wall,
> Looking as if she were alive. I call
> That piece a wonder, now: Fra Pandolf's hands
> Worked busily a day, and there she stands.
> Will 't please you sit and look at her? I said
> 'Fra Pandolf" by design, for never read
> Strangers like you that pictured countenance,
> The depth and passion of its earnest glance,
> But to myself they turned …..
>
> Browning (1812-1889): *My Last Duchess*

The form doesn't matter. The poem is a poem for reasons that will be clear, hopefully, by the end of this journey. The paragraph destroys the couplet form, but then the couplet form in the poem is destroyed already by the heavy enjambment that forces anyone saying it, or reading it, to run one line into the next without a pause because the sense prevents any pause.

So enough of structure and form. Others have written extensively on verse structure, but form is not intrinsic to poetry, so the journey can move next to the comparisons that explain and clarify – or confuse – a reader: the figures of speech.

8

Figures of Speech

Figures of speech are comparisons that form a characteristic of traditional poetry, and occur in varying degrees of elaboration. To make their point they must be understood. Figures of speech clarify what a poet is saying by comparing what is less well known to what is familiar. The two basic forms discussed here are the *simile* and the *metaphor*. Those are sufficient for this journey.

Simile

The simile selects a quality shared by two things, and compares that quality in the two things using the words "like" or "as". Almost all similes answer "How?" or "How much?" through the quality compared.

> Day after day, day after day,
> We stuck, nor breath, nor motion;
> As idle as a painted ship
> Upon a painted ocean.
> > Coleridge (1772-1834): *The Rime of the Ancient Mariner*

The ship becalmed at sea is compared to a painting – with all the sense of unreality that goes with a painted ship on a painted ocean. The quality shared by the two subjects is "idle". So the degree of idleness forms the basis of comparison.

> The Assyrian came down like the wolf on the fold
> And his cohorts were gleaming with purple and gold,
> And the sheen of their spears was like stars on the sea
> Where the blue wave rolls nightly on deep Galilee.
>> Byron (1788-1824): *The Destruction of Sennacherib*

The descent of the Assyrian army on the unprepared Israelites is compared to a wolf attacking a sheepfold. It is a very neat way of saying a great deal while saying very little. In this simile, the qualities of cruelty and helplessness are implied through the words "wolf" and "fold". There is another simile in line 3 involving the shining quality of "sheen" shared by water and stars.

The simile usually uses an overt signal of comparison – "like" or "as" – but sometimes it may only imply them while remaining a simile:

> And now there came both mist and snow,
> And it grew wondrous cold;
> And ice mast-high came floating by
> As green as emerald.
>> Coleridge (1772-1834): *The Rime of the Ancient Mariner*

In the third line, "mast-high" is short for "as high as a mast".

The epic simile is a form used by Homer in both the *Iliad* and the *Odyssey*. It has been imitated from Homer, through Virgil in the *Aeneid*, down to Milton in Paradise Lost, where in Book I, he compares the fallen angels on the lake of Hell to fallen leaves or scattered marsh grass:

> Angel Forms, who lay entranced
> Thick as autumnal leaves that strow the brooks
> In Vallombrosa, where the Etrurian shades
> High over-arched embower; or scattered sedge
> Afloat, when with fierce winds Orion armed
> Hath vexed the Red-Sea coast, whose waves o'erthrew
> Busiris and his Memphian chivalry,
> While with perfidious hatred they pursued
> The sojourners of Goshen, who beheld
> From the safe shore their floating carcases
> And broken chariot-wheels.

John Milton (1608-1674) *Paradise Lost Book I*

Epic simile also occurs in The Lord of the Rings – a prose work, though the simile reads very much like poetry:

> As when death smites the swollen brooding thing that inhabits their crawling hill and holds them all in sway, ants will wander witless and purposeless and then feebly die, so the creatures of Sauron, orc or troll or beast spell-enslaved, ran hither and thither mindless; and some slew themselves, or cast themselves in pits, or fled wailing back to hide in holes and dark lightless places far from hope.

J.R.R. Tolkien (1892-1973)
LotR vi: The Field of Cormallen

Epic similes, extending as they do over several lines, are often full of reference to Greek and Roman mythology, and usually interfere with the flow of both action and meaning which they interrupt to elaborate their long, long point.

<u>Metaphor</u>

Beyond the overt comparison of simile lies the more subtle, often hidden, comparison of metaphor. In his essay <u>*Here Lies Miss Groby*</u>, James Thurber (1894-1961) deals humorously with the deadly process of identifying metaphor without examining either its function, or an evaluation of gains or losses in its use. Some of that work has to be considered as it relates to poetry, because a metaphor is not an event; it is a process of clarification.

With metaphor, signal words similar to "like" or "as" are abandoned. Everyday speech is full of metaphor which is accepted without a thought. With the threat of a hurricane, the newspaper may print, *"Will Hurricane Bill bruise or bluster?"* Most people accept the metaphor without question or recognition.

Run is an example of a metaphor used so often that the word had to be given 89 different definitions in the Oxford English Dictionary, and many of the definitions have up to 8 different subdivisions. When a metaphor gets so overused, it loses its force as comparison.

Here are examples where metaphor starts openly and fades through subtlety.

> The president's mother, Mrs. Smith, was a cat.
> The president's mother, stroking his cloak with sheathed claws, said "Nice!"
> The president's mother purred, "Nice!"

The first statement is simple metaphor; the second implies a comparison with "sheathed claws"; the third suggests the comparison through one word: "purred".

In Richard III (IV-iv) by Shakespeare, Margaret of Anjou, speaking to Richard's mother, starts a metaphor for the villainous king that runs for 32 lines:

> From forth the kennel of thy womb hath crept
> A hell-hound that doth hunt us all to death:
> That dog, that had his teeth before his eyes,
> To worry lambs and lap their gentle blood...

It concludes:

> Cancel his bond of life dear God I pray,
> That I may live to say, "The dog is dead!"

Where epic simile stops the action and interrupts the flow and meaning of a poem, extended metaphor, as in this instance, enriches both action and meaning, clarifying as it goes.

To move on from basic metaphor, there are four subdivisions, each with its own name and distinct characteristics. Since this journey towards poetry moves from fact-dominated material to feeling-dominated matter, it is important to understand these concrete concepts now in order to master more abstract ones later.

Personification presents animals or objects as though they are human beings.

> With how sad steps, O Moon, thou climb'st the skies!
> How silently, and with how wan a face!
> What may it be that even in heavenly place
> That busy archer with his sharp arrows tries?
>   Sir Philip Sidney (1554-1586): *Astrophel and Stella xxxi*

The moon is addressed like a person – a sad one. Like metaphor, personification can be implied, and may be missed because it doesn't strain the imagination.

> The prosecuting attorney allowed the evidence to speak for itself.

Evidence cannot speak, but here it is presented as though it can talk like a person.

Allegory uses groups of characters – human and non-human – to represent ideas or abstract qualities like virtues and vices. Fable is a specific form of allegory where animals are represented with human foibles in human situations, and each fable ends with a lesson or a moral:

> The Grasshopper sang the summer away,
> And hopped about the land all day.
> But when cold winds began to blow,
> And grey clouds threatened sleet and snow,
> He said, "I'll visit the Ant to see
> If she will show me charity."…..etc.

As opposed to the simple form in fable, Spenser built the six books of his Faerie Queen on allegory to deal with six moral virtues. Spenser dramatized each virtue through extended action. Without allegory it would be very dry theological writing. When virtues like holiness, courage, and chastity are treated as people, they live beyond the ideas that they represent by illustrating those virtues in action. The story thus gains a depth and importance beyond what would otherwise have been simply a puzzle. There is, however, a down side. Once the allegorical creatures are "solved", many allegories lose their interest.

Metonymy is a form of metaphor where the characteristic of an object stand for the whole object.

> There was a sound of revelry by night,
> And Belgiums' capital had gathered then
> Her *beauty* and her *chivalry*, and bright
> The lights shone o'er fair women and brave men.
> > Byron (1788-1824): *Childe Harold*

Metonymy takes the characteristic of women (beauty) and men (chivalry) and speaks of them as if they are people, as Byron explains in the following line. In passing, notice that "Belgium's capital had gathered" is personification.

The American National Anthem has metonymy sung every day and no one considers it or thinks about it:

> The land of the *free* and the home of the *brave*…

In this country-western song by Garth Brooks, the entire stanza is metonymy with all the characteristics of rodeo listed:

> Well, it's bulls and blood   It's dust and mud
> > It's the roar of a Sunday crowd
> It's the white in the knuckles It's the gleam in the buckles
> > And the hope to win the next go 'round
> It's boots and chaps   It's cowboy hats
> > It's spurs and latigo
> It's the ropes and the reins   And the joys and the pains
> > And they call the thing "rodeo".

Synecdoche is a form of metaphor where, instead of the characteristic standing for the whole thing, now a part of the thing stands for the whole – often taught as "container for the thing contained."

> All *hands* on deck. We see a fleet of forty *sails*.

In the first example, part of a sailor, the hand, is used for the man. In the second, a part of a ship, the sail, represents the ship itself.

The difference between metonymy and synecdoche may seem subtle, but confusion can result if the types of metaphor are mixed. Here is a famous example:

> The hand that rocked the cradle kicked the bucket.

The "hand" is clearly mother: synecdoche where part (hand) stands for the whole (mother); "kicked the bucket" is a metaphor for death. The two cannot be linked. Either (a) the hand that rocked the cradle died, or (b) the mother kicked the bucket.

Sometimes metaphorical language passes beyond metaphor and creates puzzlement and awe. This type of material beyond metaphor is symbolism and the words create a shadowy world where what is meant lies far beyond anything that the words say. Since symbolism can be both a figure of speech and a poetic technique, a detailed explanation forms Appendix I.

The next stage in this journey towards poetry moves from what has to be understood to a region where sound gradually makes itself more important than the sense of what is said.

9

Rhythm

There is a relationship and resonance between dance, music, and poetry. The poet Richard Outram (1930-2006) claimed to have heard that music was great the closer it came to dance, and poetry was great the closer it came to music. In considering links between music and poetry – between sound and language – there are qualities that apply to both like rhythm, structure, melody, modality or mood, and harmony between sound and sense,.

Poetry's first characteristic shared with music is rhythm. Just as there are names for musical rhythmic forms – waltz, cha-cha, samba – the Greeks named the poetic feet and prescribed the number of feet to a line. Having borrowed the beat, poets adapted language to rhythms which they named. A listener can respond to the rhythms of poetry without understanding the language or knowing technical names of poetic feet, the building blocks of rhythm.

The feet and the names of the feet derive from Latin and Greek poetry, where syllables were long or short. So the scansion in classical languages was quantitative based on the length of syllables. Scansion in English poetry is based on stresses in reading or pronunciation. As a result, the transfer of the names for feet in English (stress-based) founded on classical feet (quantitative based) is imperfect. Stress is based on pronunciation; there will always be discussion and argument about the shape of a poetic foot. But the names for poetic feet have a long history of use, and are important, because they confer a kind of mastery that technical knowledge gives to a scientist. And since discussion of poetry moves from what can be known and verbalized toward a vague ineffable, it is best, as was explained before, to know and build on whatever solid foundation is available.

Syllables can be either stressed or unstressed. Stressed syllables can be marked thus / , and the unstressed like this - . Another way to mark them is to set off the stressed syllables in bold font, and leave the unstressed syllable in normal font. The method used here will be to pre-mark the stressed syllable with the stress mark mentioned above / and to set off the stressed syllable in bold font.

> A-/**long**   the /**line**   of /**smo** - ky /**hills**
> The /**crim** - son /**for** - est /**stands**
>> Bliss Carman (1861-1921): *Indian Summer*

For a discussion of the feet, the stressed and unstressed marks (/ and -) will be used to show the structure of the foot as well as the word sounds **dah** and di.

2-Syllable Feet

There are four 2-syllable feet arranged here in skeleton form:

(a)   - /   iamb or iambic foot,   (di **dah**)

(b) / -   trochee or trochaic foot   **(dah** di)
(c) / /   spondee or spondaic foot   **(dah dah)**
(d) - -   pyrrhic foot   (di di)

(a) The iambic foot (- /   di **dah**) is the commonest foot in English. Chaucer in the fourteenth century, and Shakespeare in the 16-17th century wrote the bulk of their poetry in that foot. and it sounds almost like normal English speech. Five in a row form what is called "the English line."

> That /**time** of /**year**   thou /**mayst**   in /**me**   be-/**hold**
> When /**yel**l - ow /**leaves**   or /**none**   or /**few**   do /**hang**
> U-/**pon** those /**boughs**   which /**shake** a-/**gainst**   the /**cold**
> Bare /**ru** - ined /**choirs**   where /**late**   the /**sweet**   birds /**sang**
> Shakespeare (1564-1616): *Sonnet # 73*

Many people might add stresses in the last line at foot 1 and foot 5.

> /**Bare** /**ru** - ined /**choirs**   where /**late**   the /**sweet** /**birds** /**sang**

But basically these are five-foot iambic lines.

(b) The trochaic foot (/ -   **dah** di) is difficult to sustain in English, where the language wants to end on a strong beat. *The Song of Hiawatha*, however, maintains trochaic feet throughout its epic length.

> /**By** the   /**shores** of   /**Git**-chee   /**Gu**-mee
> /**By** the   /**shi**-ning   /**big**-sea - /**Wa**-ters
> /**Stood** the   /**wig**-wam   /**of** No - /**ko** - mis
> /**Daugh**ter   /**of** the   **moon** No - /**ko** - mis.
> Longfellow (1807-1882): *The Song of Hiawatha*

Few other poets have attempted to sustain trochaic metre over any long poems.

(c) The spondaic foot (/ / dah dah) occurs less frequently. Some normal words like "blindfold" and "parchment" are spondees. The most famous one in English ends the first stanza of *La Belle Dame Sans Merci* by Keats (1795-1821):

> The /**sedge**   is /**wi** - thered /**from**   the /**lake**
> And /**no**   /<u>**birds /sing**</u>.

That last foot brings the stanza lumbering to a halt. Robert Francis (1902-1987) wrote his *Silent Poem* in spondees, four to a line – a rare form:

> /**back**/**road,** /**leaf**/**mold,** /**stone**/**wall,** /**chip**/**munk**
> /<u>**un**-der-/**brush**</u>, /**grape**/**vine,** /**wood**/**chuck,** /**shad**/**blow**
> /**wood**/**smoke,** /**cow**/**barn,** /**hon**-ey-/**suck**-le, /**wood**/**pile**
> /**saw**/**horse,** /**buck**/**saw,** /**out**/**house,** /**well**/**sweep** etc.

The procession of spondaic words presents a journey to a house, into a house, and then on to an undefined destination. The word underlined is an example of a rare 3-syllable foot called the amphimacer consisting of a stressed, an unstressed, and a stressed (/ - / **dah** di **dah**), but the pervasive meter of the poem is spondaic.

(d) The pyrrhic foot (- -   di di) exists only as a name for identification. A word that has a natural pyrrhic foot is ri-/**dic** - u-lous – marked - /   - - . There is an iambic foot followed by a pyrrhic. No poems are written in pyrrhic feet. It is simply a foot that is unattached to anything else, and, of course, must have a name.

3-Syllable Feet

This table shows the 8 ways of placing strong and weak beats in groups of 3.

(a)	- - / anapest or anapestic foot	(di di **dah**)
(b)	/ - - dactyl or dactylic foot	(**dah** di di)
(c)	- / - amphibrach or amphibrachic foot	(di **dah** di)
(d)	- / / bacchius or bacchic foot	(di **dah dah**)
(e)	/ / - antibacchius or antibacchic foot	(**dah dah** di)
(f)	/ - / amphimacer or cretic foot	(**dah** di **dah**)
(g)	/ / / molossus or molossic foot	(**dah dah dah**)
(h)	- - - I'm unaware of a name for this foot.	(di di di)

(a) The anapestic foot or anapest (- - /   di di **dah**) is commonly used for swift movement. It ends with a downbeat, but it starts with a double upbeat.

> The A-/**ssyr** - ian came /**down** like the /**wolf** on the /**fold**
> And his /**co** - horts were /**glea** - ming with /**pur** - ple and /**gold**
> And the /**sheen** of their /**spears** was like /**stars** on the /**sea**
> Where the /**blue** wave rolls /**night** - ly on /**deep** Gall-i-/**lee**
> Byron (1788-1824): *The Destruction of Sennacherib*

While this foot emphasizes every 3rd syllable, there may be reasons in some lines to vary this with an extra stress (/), for example – his /**co-**/**horts** – , and perhaps in the fourth line – the /**blue** /**wave** – , but the scansion presented is adequate.

(b) The dactylic foot or dactyl (/ - - **dah** di di) is like the trochee (/ -) only the unaccented syllable is doubled.

> /**Come** with me, /**fo**-llow me, /**swift** as a /**moth**,
> /**Ere** the /**wood**-doves /**wa**-ken.
> Marjorie Pickthall (1883-1922): *The Pool*

The mixture of metres after the first line illustrates the difficulty most poets find in writing dactylic feet for any length of time in English. The dactyl is the epic foot used by Homer in both *The Iliad* and *The Odyssey*, and by the Latin poet Virgil in *The Aeneid*. Their dactylic hexametres (6 feet to the line) had many rules:

Rule 1:   A pause had to occur in the 3rd foot after either the 1st or 2nd syllable:
either / ( ) - - or / - ( ) - . This was called the *"caesural pause" marked* ( ).

Rule 2:   The dactyl / - - could be replaced by a spondee / / (one stressed syllable could replace the two unstressed ones)

Rule 3:   The 5th foot **had to be** a dactyl / - - .

Rule 4:   The 6th or final foot **had to be** a trochee / - , or more properly, a catalectic foot – a foot from which a short unstressed syllable had been cut.

As was mentioned, Latin and Greek scansion was quantitative, based on long and short syllables. English scansion, in contrast, is based on stressed and unstressed syllables. Despite difficulties, Longfellow (1807-1882) adapted this metre to his epic *Evangeline*. A double bracket ( ) will show the caesural pause.

/**In** the A - /**ca**-dian /**land**, () on the   /**shores** of the   /**Ba**-sin of   /**Mi**-nas

/**Dis**-tant, se - /**clu**-/**ded**,   **still,** () the   /**lit-**/**tle**   /**vill**-age of   /**Grand** Pré

/**Lay** in the /**fruit-**/**ful**   /**vall**-ey.() Vast   /**mea-**/**dows** /**stretched** to the   /**east**-ward.

/**Giv**-ing the   /**vill**-age its   /**name**, () /**and**   /**pas**-ture to /**flocks** without /**num**ber.

Longfellow successfully wrote one epic (_Evangeline_) in classic dactylic hexameter, and another epic (_Hiawatha_) in trochaic tetrameter. But both poems finally sound forced; a listener unconsciously hears _Evangeline_ in anapests (- - /) and _Hiawatha_ in iambs (- /).

(c) The amphibrachic foot or amphibrach (- / - di **dah** di) is rare to find as a basic metre throughout a poem. The desire to land on a strong beat often converts the amphibrach, like the dactyl, into an anapest. Browning (1812-1889) begins successfully with amphibrachic metre in _How They Brought the Good News:_

> I /**sprang** to   the /**stir**-rup,   and **Jo**-ris,   and **he**;
> I /**gall**-oped,   Dirck /**gall**-oped,   we /**gall**-oped   all /**three**;
> 'Good /**speed**!' cried   the /**watch**, as   the /**gate**-bolts   un-/**drew**;
> 'Speed!' /**ech**-oed   the /**wall** to   us /**gall**op - ing /**through**;
> Be-/**hind** shut   the /**pos**-tern,   the /**lights** sank   to /**rest,**
> And /**in**-to   the /**mid**-night   we **gall**-oped   a-/**breast.**

Most poems in English, if they are not iambic or anapestic, use a mixture of feet, but favour those ending with a downbeat. The four other 3-syllable feet will be listed, but they don't sustain an entire poem; they occur only as an occasional foot in a line. A word or two will illustrate.

(d) The bacchic foot or bacchius (- / /   di **dah dah**) has a weak syllable followed by two stressed ones. Examples in language: you /**can't** /**go**   it /**won't** /**do**

(e) The antibacchic foot or antibacchius (/ / -   **dah dah** di) is also rare in poetry. Examples from language might be: /**stop** /**try**-ing   /**crop** /**sha**-ring

(f) The cretic foot (called amphimacer) (/ - / **dah** di **dah**) again is rare as a basic poetic metre, but examples might be: /**Out** you /**go** /**hipp** - o - /**drome**. Here are five of the amphimacers from *Silent Poem* quoted above by Robert Francis:

> /**butt**-er-/**milk**, /**can**-dle-/**stick**, /**butt**-er-/**cup**, /**thun**-der-/
> **storm**, and /**stee**-ple-/**bush.**

(g) The molossus (/ / / **dah dah dah**) has three stressed syllables. The Oxford English Dictionary, noting its rarity, gives only one example: /**for** - /**give** - /**ness**. Here are other examples of molossus:

> /**Ne'er /tell /me**   of /**glo**-ries se/**rene**-ly a/**dor**-ning
> The /**close**   of our /**day,**   the calm /**eve**   of our /**night;**
> /**Give /me /back,**   /**give /me /back**   the wild /**fresh** -
> ness of /**mor**-ning,
> Her /**clouds**   and her /**tears**   are worth /**eve** - ning's best
> /**light.**
>
> Thomas Moore (1779-1852) *I Saw From the Beach*

The opening command and the repeated plea in the third line force readers to give equal emphasis to all syllables.

1-Syllable Feet

Obviously there are only 2 ways of writing a one-syllable foot, and there is no poem that will be written in one-syllable feet.

(a) The one-syllable foot that is a weak beat (- di) will be called "an extra syllable". There is no poem constructed with this metre. Here is an example occurring at the end of a line:

And he /**sank**   to the /**floor**   with a /**shud**   -   <u>der</u>

The final syllable   -der- is outside the anapest, and is called "an extra syllable".

(b)The catalectic foot or catalect (/   **dah**) is a strong beat. In Greek and Latin poetry, the term "catalect" or "catalectic foot" was used to describe the foot at the end of a dactylic or trochaic line where a weak syllable was left out.

/**Take** your   /**cap** - tive   /**down** the   /**stair**.

The last foot "stair" is catalectic because the weak syllable to follow is absent.

In <u>*Break, Break, Break*</u> by Tennyson (1809-1892), ignore the first line and go to the rest of the stanza. The poem is in trimetre – three feet in each line. So here are the 2nd, 3rd, and 4th lines

On thy /**cold**   /**grey** /**stones**   /**O** /**sea**
                                    (1 anapest + 2 spondees)
And I /**would**   that my /**tongue**   could /**u**-tter
                                    (2 anapests + 1 amphibrach)
The /**thoughts**   that a-/**rise**   in /**me**
                                    (1 iamb, 1 anapest, 1 iamb)

Each line has three beats – and three feet – of varying lengths. And the first line?

/**Break,**   /**break,**   /**break**
                                    (3 one-syllable feet)

These are three catalectic feet, they are not a molossus. A rhythmic person knows at once that these are three feet, and would have to be set to three bars of music.

Length of Line is given by the number of feet, or by the number of syllables:

1 foot	monometer
2 feet	dimeter
3 feet	trimeter
4 feet	tetrameter
5 feet	pentameter
6 feet	hexameter
7 feet	heptameter
8 feet	octameter

Beyond that, lines are usually broken up. Iambic pentameter is called "the English line" and iambic hexameter (12 syllables) is the alexandrine or "French line".

When the number of syllables is used to specify the length of line, the designation is as follows:

1 syllable	monosyllabic
2 syllables	disyllabic
3 syllables	trisyllabic
4 syllables	tetrasyllabic
5 syllables	pentasyllabic
6 syllables	hexasyllabic
7 syllables	heptaxyllabic
8 syllables	octosyllabic
10 syllables	decasyllabic
12 syllables	dodecasyllabic

Few have danced to poetry. Edith Sitwell for her *Façade* wrote many musical forms as poems. Among them were a waltz, foxtrot, and hornpipe. The composer William Walton wrote a musical accompaniment. Here is the Polka:

> **Tra La La La**
> **Tra La**-la **La La**
> **Tra La**-la **La**-la **La**-la **La La La**
> See me dance the polka
> Said Mr. Wagg like a bear,
> In my top hat and my whiskers that
> **Tra**-la-la-la trap the fair. Etc.
>
> Edith Sitwell (1887-1964) *Façade*

Listening to poetry set to music, a listener learns two aspect of poetry that only accompanying music can make clear: the pause and the rest. A problem lies in the links between music and poetry. The English line of Chaucer, Shakespeare and Milton (iambic pentameter or decasyllabic) may be mapped in this way:

$$- / \; - / \; - / \; - / \; - / \quad \text{or} \quad \text{di } \textbf{dah} \; \text{di } \textbf{dah} \; \text{di } \textbf{dah} \; \text{di } \textbf{dah} \; \text{di } \textbf{dah}.$$

Each line starts with a weak syllable (-) and concludes with a strong syllable (/). Poets and readers have no problem, but the musician starts with a big problem. The line starts with an upbeat which lies outside the first bar. A musician solves it by placing the first syllable before the first bar, and then writes the line in three bars, two feet to each bar. In the third bar, he places a rest as long as one foot, and places the upbeat for the next line at the end of the third bar. Here it is scanned in skeleton form with the musical rest bracketed in bold font and underlined:

$$- \qquad / \; - / \; - \qquad / \; - / \; - \qquad / \; \underline{\textbf{(-/)}} \; - $$
$$\qquad / \; - / \; - \qquad / \; - / \; - \qquad / \; \underline{\textbf{(-/)}} \; - $$

And here it is marked in *Sonnet 73* by Shakespeare (1564-1616)

that /**time** of /**year** thou   /**mayst** in /**me** be   -
     /**hold** (di **dah**) when
/**yell** - ow /**leaves** or   /**none** or /**few** do
     /**hang** (di-**dah**) u –
/**pon** those /**boughs** which   /**shake** a-/**gainst** the
     /**cold** (di-**dah**) bare
/**ru** - ined /**choirs** /where   /**late** the /**sweet** birds
     /**sang** (di-**dah**)

Between each line a musician requires a rest the length of one foot because there are only 5 beats to the line – an uneven number. The musician must place the first syllable of the next line at the end of his third bar, thus removing that first syllable from the next line. A musician can spell out what is being done with rests and bar lines; a poet, lacking those diacritical marks, can't indicate pauses and rests, but must count on the words, their pronunciation, and the musicality of the reader to sense and give these pauses and rests.

Rhythm lives on the shoreline between the Land of Sense where meaning is important, and the Sea of Sound where the music of the language is as important as the sense, and in some cases exceeds the importance of the sense.

Many of the characteristics of poetry which were borrowed from music can be heard and appreciated by a person who doesn't understand the language. Some of these effects like alliteration, rhyme, consonance and assonance exist just as sound without meaning being necessary. These musical uses of language are called "Poetic Devices", and a discussion of them moves the journey to the edge of the Sea of Sound.

10

Poetic Devices

Poetic devices use the sounds of words to enhance their emotional impact and echo the sense of what is said. With poetic devices, poetry approaches the harmony and melody of music. A listener does not need to understand the language in order to appreciate the musicality of a poem. Here are the common sound-devices which have names.

(a) Repetition is the simplest device for making an emotional point. It appears in early poetry like the border ballads:

> O where have you been, Lord Randal my son?
> And where have you been, my handsome young man?
> I have been at the greenwood; mother, make my bed soon,
> For I'm wearied with hunting and fain would lie down.
>
> And who met you there, Lord Randal my son?
> And who met you there; my handsome young man?
> O I met with my true-love; mother, make my bed soon,
> For I'm wearied with hunting and fain would lie down.
>
> Traditional Ballad: *Lord Randal*

The repetition continues throughout the ballad to Lord Randal's death.

In this next example, repetition transforms the statement in the third line to a metaphor of life-and-death in the fourth line;

> The woods are lovely, dark, and deep,
> But I have promises to keep,
> And miles to go before I sleep,
> And miles to go before I sleep.

> Robert Frost (1874-1963)
> *Passing by Woods on a Snowy Eve*

(b) Alliteration occurs when words start with the same consonant sound or, more precisely, when the first accented syllables of words start with the same consonant sound. Examples will make the device clear:

> When the hounds of spring are on winter's traces,
> The **mother of months, in meadow** or plain
> Fills the shadows and windy places
> With **lisp of leaves** and **ripple of rain**

> Swinburne (1837-1909) *Atalanta in Calydon*

Note that alliteration involves the same sound, not the same letter. In the words, "be**Fore** the **Fire**" the alliteration is on "f". Although "f" is not the first letter in "before", it is the first letter in the first accented syllable as with "In**Sipid Cider**" which has alliteration with the same sounds in "s" and "c". Similarly "**F**ine **PH**rases" has the sound, not the same letters.

Alliteration was important to Anglo-Saxon poets who wrote in half-lines. Each pair alternated consonant-alliteration with what they heard as vowel-alliteration. There is nothing like it in traditional English poetry.

(c) Rhyme occurs when the strong beat in a foot is repeated with a change in the first consonant of that strong beat. It occurs usually at the end of lines, but it may be internal also. Rich rhyme would be "June – Moon". Pope wrote in heroic couplets where each pair of lines rhymes:

> Heaven from all creatures hides the Book of Fate,
> All but the page prescribed, their present state:
> From brutes what men, from men what spirits know:
> Or who could suffer Being here below?
>
> Pope (1688-1744): *Essay on Man – Part 3*

Variants of rich rhyme like "June-moon" can be assonantal rhyme when the vowel sounds rhyme and the consonants don't. Here are the first four lines of a Garth Brooks song *Two of a Kind, Working on a Full House*:

> She's my Lady Luck and I'm her Wildcard Man
> Together we're a-building up a real hot hand;
> We live out in the country and she's my little Queen of the
>   South:
> We're two of a kind, workin' on a full house.

"Man-hand" and "South-house" have vowels which rhyme but not the consonants.

Another variant is consonantal rhyme where the consonants rhyme but the vowels don't. Here are the first four lines of stanza 2 in Keats' *Ode to Autumn*:

> Who has not seen Thee oft amid thy store?
> Sometime whoever looks abroad may find
> Thee sitting careless on a granary floor,
> Thy hair soft-lifted by the winnowing wind...

The words "find-wind" have the consonants rhyming but not the vowels.

In the following example, alliteration, rhyme, and internal rhyme create a rich musical effect.

> The fair breeze blew, the white foam flew,
> The furrow followed free;
> We were the first that ever burst
> Into that silent sea.
> Coleridge (1772-1834): *The Rime of the Ancient Mariner*

That is about as musical as poetry can get, and though sound almost overpowers sense, a reader or listener can see and hear what is being said.

(d) Consonance is the use of similar consonant sounds to bind lines together and imitate the sound of what is discussed Alliteration is an obvious examples, but tongue-twisters also play with similar consonant sounds.

> She sells seashells by the seashore

This tongue-twister is full of unvoiced sibilant sounds both simple and complex. Here is an example from poetry where the nasal sounds m-n-ng and the voiced s(z) sounds bind the lines together.

The moan of doves in immemorial elms,
And murmuring of innumerable bees.

   Tennyson (1809-1894): *Come Down O Maid*

(e) Assonance is the use of the same vowels in lines to bind them together. Here the "a" and "o" vowel sounds with the consonance of "l" hold the lines together.

Alone, alone, all all alone,
Alone on a wide, wide, sea;

  Coleridge (1772-1834): *The Rime of the Ancient Mariner*

Edith Sitwell (1887-1964) chose a line from her suite *Façade* to demonstrate the gradual fronting of the vowel sound **a**:

"Sally, Mary, Mattie, what's the matter? Why cry?"

She heard a movement of the vowel "**a**" from the mid-palate to the front in "Sally, Mary, Mattie," and "matter", ending with the fronted diphthongs in "Why cry?" . There she felt the y-sounds in "why cry" as "aee", and they took what she called "a high leap into the air". To sound-sensitive people like her, the vowel music of assonance is distinct.

  The patterns and the music of assonance are what a good singer will follow. The vowels allow a column of air to be inflected by the singing voice. On those inflections, consonantal interruptions occupy as little time as possible.

(f) Onomatopoeia occurs when a poet uses sounds without meaning, to echo either movement or appearance. An example occurs in the *Trolley Song* (1944):

Clang, clang, clang went the trolley
Ding, ding, ding went the bell
Zing, zing, zing went my heartstrings
From the moment I saw him I fell
Chug, chug, chug went the motor
Bump, bump, bump went the brake
Thump, thump, thump went my heartstrings
When he smiled I could feel the car shake

Blane and Martin (1944)

The words in bold font imitate noises that the named objects would make. The words in onomatopoeia may be sounds that are non-words.

(g) Imitative Harmony uses words to present the movement spoken of in sound:

Dry clashed his armor in the icy caves
And barren chasms, and all to left and right,
The bare black cliffs clanged round him as he based
His feet on juts of slippery crag that rang
Sharp-smitten with the dint of armèd heels.

Tennyson (1809-1894): Morte d'Artur (186-190)

These five lines (186-190) clatter with unvoiced consonants like "clashed-caves-chasms-black-cliffs-clanged-based-feet-juts-crag-sharp-smitten-dint" imitating the sound of a man in armor striding over the mountain.

(h) Tone Color uses word-sounds to paint a picture. Here are the next two lines:

And on a sudden, lo! the level lake,
And the long glories of the winter moon.

Tennyson (1809-1894): Morte d'Artur (191-192)

These two lines (191-192) paint the peaceful beauty of the lake with long vowels and voiced consonants and nasals.

Imitative harmony, through the sound of words and the use of consonants with long or short vowels, speaks to the ear; tone color, using the same sounds, speaks to the eye.

For those sensitive to the music of language, the change between the imitative harmony in the first five lines (186-190) and the tone color of the last two lines (191-192) is breath-taking, and line 7 is magical with liquids – l-r, the nasals – m-n-ng, and long vowel sounds that sing in the words – *long, glories,* and *moon.*

Just as there are people tone-deaf to music – people to whom melody and changes in pitch mean little – so also there are people tone-deaf to language – people to whom language has only meaning and the sound is lost. They are deaf to the change between line 190 and line 191, and deaf to the miracle of line 192. For them the meaning is all that exists in these lines.

(i) Pitch and Tone of Voice affect the musical quality of poetry. In his essays, *The Cutting of an Agate*, Yeats (1865-1939) wrote in the first chapter about hearing his poetry recited by a woman who strummed a psaltery as she spoke. He remarked on her speaking voice moving between tones – musical tones – though she didn't sing, chant, or intone. Since the speaking voice moves within a range of definable tones, a poem might be "scored" or set to music using that range of tones. There are many examples in that essay of his own poems scored that way.

Most people never think of voice as musical instrument when it speaks, but poets have always been aware of it, and early poets chanted or intoned their poems.

(j) Elocutionary Effects demonstrate *how* something is to be said or read. For the elocutionist, *pitch* and *volume* turn the voice into a musical instrument like the voice mentioned above. Choral poetry depends on the same two effects – pitch and volume. Two other elocutionary effects are *pauses* and the *rests*. Those four – pitch, volume, pauses and rests – are like the instructions in a musical score for volume (from *piano* to *forte*), with pauses – the fermata (the circled dot above a note) and the rests.

Lines from Shakespeare's *Richard III iv-4* can illustrate well elocutionary effects with pitch and tone of voice. Here is a scene with old Queen Margaret of Anjou, widow of King Henry VI, as principal speaker. The Duchess of York, and the Duchess's daughter-in-law, Elizabeth Woodville, widow of King Edward IV have come to join Margaret of Anjou in Westminster Abbey, seeking sanctuary. Richard III, the Duchess of York's son, has just killed his two nephews, Elizabeth's two children, the little princes in the Tower of London. Margaret of Anjou is speaking to Elizabeth Woodville with all the hatred she felt for that young wife of Edward IV, usurper of the throne from Henry VI, Margaret's husband.

> I called thee once "vain flourish of my fortune";
> I called thee then "poor shadow, painted queen" –
> The presentation of but what I was,
> The flattering index of a direful pageant,
> One heaved a-high to be hurled down below,
> A mother only mocked with two fair babes,
> A dream of what thou wast, a garish flag,

> To be the aim of every dangerous shot;
> A sign of dignity, a breath, a bubble,
> A queen in jest, only to fill the scene.

In the next lines, questions break some of the line but leave the metre intact. How long should the pause after each question be?

> Where is thy husband now? Where be thy brothers?
> Where be thy two sons? Wherein dost thou joy?
> Who sues and kneels and says, 'God save the queen'?
> Where be the bending peers that flattered thee?
> Where be the thronging troops that followed thee?
> Decline all this, and see what now thou art:

In each of the following lines there is a pause, and three problems confront the speaker: (a) how long to pause? (b) by how many tones to place the first half-line lie above the second? and (c) how long to pause at the end of each line? Each line has a balance that is almost antiphonal.

> For happy wife, a most distressed widow;
> For joyful mother, one that wails the name;
> For one being sued to, one that humbly sues;
> For queen, a very caitiff crowned with care;
> For she that scorned at me, now scorned of me;
> For she being feared of all, now fearing one;
> For she commanding all, obeyed of none.

How these lines should be said are musical as well as dramatic questions.

(k) Word Magic: Any "magic" in poetry is tied to the music of language, and the poet, sensitive to the sound of words, develops through practice the skill and art of choosing the right word. Two examples from Swinburne illustrate both music and magic:

> And in green underwood and cover
> Blossom by blossom the spring begins.
>> A.C. Swinburne (1837-1909) *Atalanta in Calydon*

Anyone may substitute a word for "blossom" – bud by bud, flower by flower, bloom by bloom, crocus by crocus – but nothing matches the original "blossom", and it is difficult to find a better description of the coming of spring.

In his poem *Laus Veneris*, the magical power rises as the lines progress:

> Ah, yet would God this flesh of mine might be
> Where air might wash and long leaves cover me;
> Where tides of grass break into foam of flowers,
> Or where the wind's feet shine along the sea.
>> A.C. Swinburne (1837-1909) *Laus Veneris*

The sound in these lines is like an exercise in unvoiced and voiced consonants: unvoiced *wh* in *where* to voiced *w* in *wind's*; voiced *d* in *wind's* to unvoiced *t* in *feet*. Another pair are the complex sibilant *sh* in *shine* and the simple sibilant *s* in *sea*. Short vowels *e* and *i* in *where* and *wind* are matched with long vowel *e* in *feet* and *sea*, and long *i* in *shine*. The combination of metaphor with tone color in the last line "Or where the wind's feet shine along the sea" create a climactic musical effect that approaches magical transformation.

The quality of composing poetry like music set Swinburne apart from other poets. The meaning in his poetry mattered less than the sound.

Before moving further down the beach on the Continent of Sense toward the Sea of Sound, I'm expanding a discussion of Imitative Harmony and Tone Color in more detail, with the full palette of consonant and vowel sounds, those shaping tools of poetry's magic.

11

The Union of Sound and Sense

'Tis not enough no harshness gives offense,
The sound must seem an echo to the sense:
> Pope (1688-1744) *Essay on Criticism: Part 2, 362-365*

<u>Imitative Harmony and Tone Color</u>

These two poetic devices pervade poetry. Imitative harmony uses the sound of words to echo the movement being described, and its principal appeal is to the ear. Tone color uses the sound of words to evoke the appearance of what is described, and its principal appeal is to the eye. Often both sight and hearing are appealed to, and the two are joined. It sounds odd to say that sounds appeal to the eye, but here is a poem by Shelley with the devices marked:

The keen stars were twinkling	} tone
And the fair moon was rising among them,	} color
Dear Jane!	}

The guitar was tinkling,	> imitative
But the notes were not sweet till you sung them	> harmony
Again.	>
As the moon's soft splendor	} tone
O'er the faint cold starlight of Heaven	} color
Is thrown,	}
So your voice most tender	> imitative
To the strings without soul had then given	> harmony
Its own.	>
The stars will awaken,	} tone
Though the moon sleep a full hour later	} color
Tonight;	}
No leaf will be shaken	> imitative
Whilst the dews of your melody scatter	> harmony
Delight.	>
Though the sound overpowers,	> imitative
Sing again, with your dear voice revealing	> harmony
A tone	>
Of some world far from ours,	- synthesis
Where music and moonlight and feeling	- in
Are one.	- thought

Shelley (1792-1822) *To Jane*

In the first three lines of the first three stanzas, the sounds of the words reflect the glitter of stars with k, t, s, and short vowels (I-1, II-2, III-1), and the calm beauty of the moon and sky with m, n, r, s(z), and long vowels (I-2, II-1, III-2). The sense appealed to is the eye and sight.

In the last three lines of the first three stanzas along with the first three lines of the last stanza, the sounds of the words

echo the guitar and a leaf (I-4-5, and III-4), and the beauty of
both the song and Jane's voice with m, n, ng (I-5-6, II-4-5-6,
III-5). The sense appealed to is the ear and hearing.

Though the same letters are used for the two devices,
imitative harmony speaks to the ear and hearing, while tone color
appeals to the eye and sight. Two questions help to distinguish
between the two devices: do I see it, or do I hear it.

Here are some other examples:

> There lies the port; the vessels puff their sails
> There gloom the dark broad seas.
>
> Tennyson (1809-1895) *Ulysses ll.44-45*

The short vowels and unvoiced consonants in the first line
(after the first foot "*There lies*") present a tonal picture of the
foreground. They contrast with the long vowels and voiced
consonants of the second line, the background of darkness,
vastness, and power. It is all tone color.

If you read the lines aloud, you hear the difference, and
if you chant or intone them, the contrast between voiced and
unvoiced becomes obvious. This explanation of the two lines
seems like overkill, but songs and symphonies are built up note
by note and instrument by instrument. In those lines, a picture
is painted letter-by-letter and sound-by-sound.

Here two lines of tone color precede one line of imitative
harmony:

> The lights begin to twinkle from the rocks,
> The long day wanes, the slow moon climbs,
> The deep moans round with many voices;
>
> Tennyson (1809-1895) *Ulysses ll.54-56*

The first line, with short vowels and unvoiced consonants, seems to sparkle before the eyes. The second line with long vowels and sounds "ng, m, n" slows down everything, and a reader can see the end of the day with moonrise. In a movement from eye to ear, the final line uses long vowels like ee, oa, ou, oi and the nasals m, n, to slow the line down even more, and you can hear the sea.

These examples demonstrate creation of sight and sound through a palette of voiced and unvoiced consonants, and of short and long vowels.   The examples demonstrate the truth of Popes Essay on Criticism:

The sound must seem an echo to the sense

A lot of practice is required to identify passages where sound mirrors sense, and to identify how the choice of words makes the difference in how a passage "looks" to the eye, and "sounds" to the ear. Clusters of unvoiced consonants and short vowels can seem to skitter across a page.

Myriads of rivulets hurrying through the lawn
Tennyson (1809-1895) *Come Down O Maid* (3rd last line)

Rachmaninov describes a violent argument between Rimsky-Korsakov who saw gold with C major, and a fellow composer who saw a different color. Readers needn't be that fastidiously discriminating, but by reading aloud and listening to series of sound like pup-pub-bub-bum-mum or tat-tad-dad-dan-nan, readers can learn to hear the appeal to both eye and ear in a poem like the following:

The splendor falls on castle walls   }
     And snowy summits old in story: } tone

The long light shakes across the lakes,   } color
     And the wild cataract leaps in glory. }
Blow, bugle, blow, set the wild echoes flying, > imitative
Blow, bugle; answer, echoes, dying, dying,   > harmony
     dying.

O hark, O hear! how thin and clear,   >
     And thinner, clearer, farther going! > all
O sweet and far from cliff and scar   > imitative
     The horns of Elfland faintly blowing! > harmony
Blow, let us hear the purple glens replying: >
Blow, bugle; answer, echoes, dying, dying,   >
     dying.

O love, they die in yon rich sky,   } tone
     They faint on hill or field or river: } color
Our echoes roll from soul to soul,   - metaphor
     And grow for ever and for ever.   - and
                                           meaning
Blow, bugle, blow, set the wild echoes flying, > imitative
And answer, echoes, answer, dying, dying,   > harmony
     dying.

                    Tennyson (1809-1895) *Song* from *The Princess*

Here, by contrast, are rats from *The Pied Piper* by Browning
(1812-1889):

Rats!   > all
They fought the dogs and killed the cats   >
And bit the babies in their cradles,   > imitative
And ate the cheeses out of the vats   >
And licked the soup from the cooks' own ladles, > harmony
Broke open the kegs of salted sprats,   >

Made nests inside men's Sunday hats	> all
And even spoiled the women's chats	>
By drowning their speaking	> imitative
With shrieking and squeaking	>
In fifty different sharps and flats.	> harmony

In both those examples, the sound echoes the sense.

Often one word will evoke hearing or sight, as in the following poem:

> Far in a western brookland
> That bred me long ago
> The poplars stand and tremble
> By pools I used to know.
>
> There, in the windless night-time,
> The wanderer, marveling why,
> Halts on the bridge to hearken
> How soft the poplars sigh.
>
> He hears: no more remembered
> In fields where I was known,
> Here I lie down in London
> And turn to rest alone.
>
> There, by the **starlit fences**,
> The wanderer halts and hears
> My soul that lingers sighing
> Above the **glimmering weirs**.
>
>   A.E. Housman (1859-1936) *A Shropshire Lad*

The first three stanzas are for the ear – imitative harmony; lines 1 and 4 of the last stanza are completely for the eye – tone color. There is a twinkle in the first line "starlit fences", magic in the last line "glimmering", and infinite sadness in the "soul that lingers sighing".

A constant exposure to the sound of poetry – reading it aloud or listening to it read – can train a person to hear and see how sound can echo sense.

12

Interlude: At the Edge of the Sea of Sound

In this geographical and metaphorical journey towards poetry, any move further away from the Land of Sense passes into the Sea where there is sound alone, or sound without sense as in ululation and moan. In the wash of the waves are poems like Swinburne's <u>Nephelidia</u>, his parody of his own alliterative foibles:

> From the depth of the dreamy decline of the dawn
> through a notable nimbus of nebulous noonshine,
> Pallid and pink as the palm of the flag-flower
> that flickers with fear of the flies as they float,
> Are the looks of our lovers that lustrously lean
> from a marvel of mystic miraculous moonshine,
> These that we feel in the blood of our blushes
> that thicken and threaten with throbs through the throat...etc.
>
> A.C. Swinburne (1837-1909) *Nephelidia*

Beyond that, in the shallows of the Sea of Sound, may lie the liquid, musical language like Tolkien's Elvish, a language which he created and then translated into English. Here are the opening lines of A Elbereth Gilthoniel from LotR:

A Elbereth Gilthoniel	O Elbereth Starkindler,
silivren penna míriel	white-glittering, slanting,
	sparkling like a jewel,
o menel aglar elenath!	the glory of the starry host!

J.R.R Tolkien (1892-1973) *Lord of the Rings*

Other invented languages lying in the shallows might be Klingon *from* Startrek, *or the language invented for the film* Avatar.

Beyond that, in the Sea of Sound, there is sound without sense, and that sound, when organized, is music; when disorganized, it is noise.

So the metaphorical journey comes to an end. The time for conclusion has come, but the conclusion will bring no surprises.

13

Conclusion

Language may be used to organize, to present, or to construct facts. These uses of language are planted firmly in the Land of Sense, and are called *prose*. As important as the journey to poetry is, so is an evaluation of that other use of language, prose. It is worth while to look backward from the beach to the Land of Sense. To understand prose helps to understand the function of poetry.

Prose generally takes one of five forms: exposition, description, narration, advocacy, and lists. Though the first four were discussed before, re- examination will help to confirm the functions of prose.

Exposition has the goals of clarity, conciseness, and coherence. Logic guides the structure, and meaning dominates this form of writing. The purpose of exposition is to explain and convince.

Description presents material appealing to the five senses. The writing must make a careful delineation of space with background, middle ground, and foreground, so that the eye may clearly see what is written. Sound, smell, taste, and touch are important depending on what is being described. The purpose of description is to locate a reader or listener in the space spoken of.

__Narration__ uses character, setting, and plot to present the people, the location and the incidents making up a story. The purpose is to create a fictional world as consistent and real as this world we live in.

__Advocacy__ tries to present a convincing point of view and to sell. Printing presses pour out rhetorical devices with slogans, jingles, jargon, and casuistry, while factories pour out exaggeration and misinformation.

Prose has its own realm of effects and devices, and their purpose is to clarify, to explain, and to create unequivocal meaning. Other rhetorical devices, as opposed to poetic devices, are comparison, contrast, hyperbole, particularization and generalization. More rhetorical devices can be found as lists on the internet.

Prose is language used to present or create facts. It is rooted in observation and reason.

In contrast to all those uses of language called "prose", language may be used to create, organize, present, or construct emotional experience. This use is rooted in emotion and imagination. Feelings and emotions dominate through sound. This use of language is called *poetry*. In our geographical metaphor, poetry lives on the beach between the Continent of Sense and the Sea of Sound.

The two forms almost always occur in all writing. Poetry must present some fact or facts on which to build its emotional experience. Prose often uses poetic figures of speech like simile and metaphor to make its points. But if a common adage may be invoked – one swallow does not make a summer – then in a similar way, one figure of speech does not convert prose into poetry, and likewise some facts do not turn poetry into prose.

Prose speaks to the head and to reason; poetry speaks to the heart and to the imagination. As has been said, most writing is a combination of the two. The *Gettysburg Address* and *Lincoln's Second Inaugural Address* mentioned at the beginning illustrate the two uses of language bound together.

Some public speeches and sermons are more poetry than prose. Some novels contain much poetry. Mary Webb, in *Precious Bane*, writes passages of poetry. Here is a description Sarn Mere, the lake near the heroine's home:

> ...but the sky that is in the mere is not the proper heavens. You see it in a glass darkly, and the long shadows of rushes go thin and sharp across the sliding stars, and even the sun and moon might be put out down there, for, times, the moon would get lost in lily leaves, and, times, a heron might stand before the sun.
>
> Mary Webb (1881-1927) *Precious Bane I-i Sarn Mere*

From the point where she says "in a glass darkly" with the reference to Pauls First Epistle to the Corinthians she is writing lyrical poetry reaching its climax in the last phrase, "times, a heron might stand before the sun."

There are other ways of presenting prose and poetry. Here is one in terms of function:

> *prose is the use of language that says what it means, and means what it says; poetry is that use of language that says what it means, but often means not only what it says but*

something different from, or more than what it says; what it says only approximates what it means.

Here is another presentation of poetry:

Poetry is the only way to express through language those things that can't be put into words.

Those things that cannot be put into words are emotional experiences. This paradoxical statement says, among other things, that when language expresses through words things that cannot themselves be put into words, then there exists the process called poetry; the product is a poem. One way language achieves that goal is with figures of speech – comparisons through similes and metaphors, to imply that a things is not just itself but also something else. Another way language achieves that goal is through poetic devices – in the combination of the precise word with specific sounds to reflect both appearance and movement. A third way is with an object or situation that creates or conveys the emotion – what is called an objective correlative.

In summary, and in very condensed form, prose is the use of language to present or communicate facts; poetry is the use of language to create or re-create emotional experience. Many people don't agree with these definitions and distinctions, but I have found them to be true up to this time.

I promised that the conclusion would bring no surprises, and that is true. At the beginning I said that I had never heard of anyone who arrived at journey's end. I don't feel that I have reached journey's end – poetry – yet!

For a long time, and particularly since the writing of this short piece, I have concluded that there is no end to the journey towards poetry. Just as there are earthquakes and tsunamis in the geographical world, so there are changes in the Land of Sense and in the Sea of Sound as their boundaries shift. The world of emotional experience, the world of poetry and music, under the nine-fold rule of the Muses, will always and forever be exciting.

Two appendixes follow. The first is an exposition of symbolism with examples. The second is a brief summary of criticism and critique for this work – this journey.

The End

APPENDIX I

Symbolism as Figure of Speech and as Technique

As was stated in the discussion of figures of speech, there are times when metaphor passes beyond itself and fills a reader or listener with puzzlement and awe. Two passages here illustrate that power. In Job (38:1-7), God speaks out of a whirlwind. He asks unanswerable questions which lie beyond all degrees of comparison, building up through verses 4, 5, and 6 to a kind of ecstasy in Verse 7.

1   Then the Lord answered Job out of the whirlwind, and said,

2   Who is this that darkeneth counsel by words without knowledge?

3   Gird up now thy loins like a man; for I will demand of thee, and answer thou me.

4   Where wast thou when I laid the foundations of the earth? declare, if thou hast understanding.

5   Who hath laid the measures thereof, if thou knowest? or who hath stretched the line upon it?

6   Whereupon are the foundations thereof fastened? or who laid the corner stone thereof;

7   When the morning stars sang together, and all the sons of God shouted for joy?

Job 38: 1-7

In the Gospel of John (6: 53-56), when Jesus Christ speaks of himself, what is said often lies beyond metaphor:

53   Verily, verily, I say unto you, Except ye eat the flesh of the Son of man, and drink his blood, ye have no life in you.

54   Whoso eateth my flesh, and drinketh my blood, hath eternal life; and I will raise him up at the last day.

55   For my flesh is meat indeed, and my blood is drink indeed.

56   He that eateth my flesh and drinketh my blood dwelleth in me and I in him

When one object in a poem or story persistently represents another, we have either allegory or extended metaphor. The word "symbolize" is often used, but this is inaccurate. Symbolism lies beyond simile, beyond metaphor with all its subdivisions, and sits at the border of meaning itself. There are three ways in which it may be considered: two ways as a figure of speech, and one way as a poetic technique.

The 1st Type of Symbolism

It appears as supranormal metaphor in the Jewish Bible. Impossible images are presented as if they are commonplace

– as elemental reality. Here are two examples, one from Isaiah and one from Daniel:

> Isa:11:6: The wolf also shall dwell with the lamb, and the leopard shall lie down with the kid; and the calf and the young lion and the fatling together; and a little child shall lead them.

Though Isaiah speaks about animals and a child, he is talking through these impossible relationships about something far beyond the creatures named.

> Daniel 7:13-14 I saw in the night visions, and, behold, one like the Son of man came with the clouds of heaven, and came to the Ancient of days and they brought him near before him.
>
> And there was given him dominion, and glory, and a kingdom, that all people, nations, and languages, should serve him: his dominion is an everlasting dominion, which shall not pass away, and his kingdom that which shall not be destroyed.

This transcends all reality. The words are a bridge to the impossible and the ineffable through vague hypnotic language.

One remarkable aspect of the imagery in both these passages is the simple elemental quality, of the language. The simpler the language, the more levels of meaning it acquires, cracking the bounds of reality and understanding.

The 2nd Type of Symbolism

It appears as transcendental metaphor in the Gospel of John. Some simple comparisons, when sustained beyond the bounds of what they say or mean, become luminous, and assume qualities and virtues that they lack completely in the prosaic world of fact. When Jesus Christ defines himself in the Gospel of John, his statements look like metaphors, but the elaboration of each definition breaks the boundary that defines metaphor, and magnifies the meaning to a plane above what is comprehensible. The definitions are then symbols rather than metaphors.

> John 4,13-14 Whosoever drinketh of this water shall thirst again: But whosoever drinketh of the water that I shall give him shall never thirst; but the water that I give shall be in him a well of water springing up into everlasting life.

This passage uses the very simplest of objects – water and thirst. But the message and promise transcend the meaning and stand against any reality that we can know or experience. A second passage contains an impossible promise whose statement itself is transcendence. No explanation is possible

> John 11,25-26 I am the resurrection, and the life: he that believeth in me, though he were dead, yet shall he live: And whosoever liveth and believeth in me shall never die.

The 3rd Type of Symbolism

Symbolism can be a poetic technique – a technique recognized in France from the middle of the 19th century by Baudelaire and his followers. It had been used before, as this example shows, but the French symbolists defined it and consciously practiced its use.

Shakespeare's Othello enters Desdemona's bedroom with a candle in the last act of the play. He plans to kill her, and says:

> Put out the light (the candle), and then put out the light
>   (Desdemona):
> If I quench thee, thou flaming minister,
> I can again thy former light restore,
> Should I repent me: – but once put out thy light,
> Thou cunning'st pattern of excelling nature,
> I know not where is that Promethean heat
> That can thy light relume. **When I have pluckt the rose**
> **I cannot give it vital growth again;**
> **It needs must wither. I'll smell it on the tree.**
> O balmy breath, that dost almost persuade
> Justice to break her sword!

The allusions are comprehensible. The metaphor of the candle for human life is powerful and tragically sad. But the statement about the rose comes out of nowhere. It is a universal statement about all roses, and about all people who have ever picked a rose. Only by continuance and context is the rose a metaphor for Desdemona. The universal statement about a rose stands abstractly – unrelated to anything preceding it. This lack of relatedness makes it more powerful as a statement about the nature of killing, and the impotence of anyone human to restore life to human or flower. Take away the 2½ line rose-passage that has been set apart in bold font, and it affects the sadness of the scene very little.

> Put out the light (the candle), and then put out the light
>   (Desdemona):
> If I quench thee, thou flaming minister,
> I can again thy former light restore,
> Should I repent me: – but once put out thy light,
> Thou cunning'st pattern of excelling nature,
> I know not where is that Promethean heat
> That can thy light relume.

> O balmy breath, that dost almost persuade
> Justice to break her sword!

Its presence, however, adds a dimension that goes beyond the words themselves, and deepens the despair in Othello at the prospect of killing.

It is the juxtaposition of the rose-lines with the rest that represents symbolist technique. Its deletion leaves great poetry; its addition creates a second and a third relationship – between Desdemona and the rose, and between the candle and the rose. For the symbolist poets, the new relationship between the candle and the rose represents their symbolist technique. Not just a second dimension, but a third.

The chorus from the song *Total Eclipse of the Heart* (Bonnie Tyler 1983) is symbolist in technique, and defies analysis.

> Once upon a time I was falling in love
> Now I'm only falling apart;
> There's nothing I can do --
> Total eclipse of the heart.

The last line is symbolism. If we remove the line, there is a state of despair; the last line adds a new metaphor, eclipse, to the two meanings of "falling". The new metaphor baffles and delights – it is vivid, exact, and impossible.

These three sets of examples represent the three ways in which the term Symbolism may be used. The ways mentioned present two types for symbolism of transcendence, and one example of symbolist technique. The first symbolism of transcendence is achieved through elemental language as in *Isaiah* and *Daniel*; the second symbolism of transcendence is arrived at through metaphor that breaks the bounds of meaning as is shown in *John's Gospel*. The third, the symbolist technique, uses the juxtaposition of two metaphors, and that juxtaposition creates a third element, and perhaps a fourth, and so on.

Symbolism stands at the edge of understanding and the border of meaning; beyond it lies what is ineffable.

If we return to the metaphor of poetry as a journey, the figures of speech sit at the high tide mark on the beach at the edge of meaning. We must understand the language to grasp the comparisons whose purpose is to clarify meaning. Symbolism sits there with the other figures of speech, but breaks meaning with impossible statements (types 1 and 2) and off-the-wall comparisons (type 3).

APPENDIX II

Criticism and Critique

The Poet's Position Relative to His Poem (and relative to his reader)

James Joyce, in his **Portrait of the Artist as a Young Man** (Section V) outlines three forms that art can take when the work of art is considered relative to the artist. These three forms can be applied to poetry. Here are the relevant passages with a brief commentary after each to relate them to poetry.

*Art necessarily divides itself into three forms progressing from one to the next. These forms are: the **lyrical form**, wherein the artist presents his image in immediate relation to himself; the **epical form**, wherein he presents his image in mediate relation to himself and to others; the **dramatic form**, wherein he presents his image in immediate relation to others.*

*The **lyrical form** is in fact the simplest verbal vesture of an instant of emotion, a rhythmical cry such as ages ago cheered on the man who pulled at the oar or dragged stones up a slope. He who utters it is more conscious of the instant of emotion than of himself as feeling it.*

Most short poetry is of this form from the time before the Horatian odes to occasional poems in magazines today. The poet stands between the subject matter and the reader, inviting the reader or listener to share the poet's emotion. And the reader or listener is very aware of the poet standing there between the poem and all readers or listeners.

*The simplest **epical form** is seen emerging out of lyrical literature when the artist prolongs and broods upon himself as the centre of an epical event and this form progresses till the centre of emotional gravity is equidistant from the artist himself and from others. The narrative is no longer purely personal. The personality of the artist passes into the narration istself, flowing round and round the persons and action like a vital sea. This progress you will see easily in that old English ballad Turpin Hero which begins in the first person and ends in the third person.*

Narrative poetry from before *The Iliad* and *Odyssey*, through *The Rime of the Ancient Mariner*, up to the present time are all epical in form. The poet is the storyteller and tells the story his way incorporating the personal viewpoint, but as narrator, he stands to the side, not between the work of art and the reader as in the lyrical mode.

*The **dramatic form** is reached when the vitality which has flowed and eddied round each person fills every person with such vital force that he or she assumes a proper and intangible esthetic life. The personality of the artist, at first a cry or a cadence or a mood, and then a fluid and lambent narrative, finally refines itself out of existence, impersonalizes itself, so to speak. The esthetic image in the dramatic form is life purified in and reprojected from the human imagination. The*

mystery of esthetic creation, like that of material creation, is
accomplished. The artist, like the God of the creation, remains
within or behind or beyond or above his handiwork, invisible,
refined out of existence, indifferent, paring his fingernails.

Examples of the dramatic form stretch from Greek Theatre up through Christopher Fry and Peter Shaffer. Robert Browning wrote many poems in the form called "dramatic monologue", as exemplified in *Andrea del Sarto*, or the cycle of dramatic monologues in *The Ring and the Book*. A dramatic monologue by Tennyson, his contemporary, exemplifies the form well in *Ulysses*, which in its 70 lines, presents a dramatic scene. Tennyson is not present; Ulysses talks. A reader learns almost nothing about the poet – only about the character talking.

It is never sufficient for a piece of writing to simply "put you there" in order to be a poem. Vivid description and excellent narrative may do that. Poetry demands the dynamism, the emotional thrill, of an arresting experience – anything from a tremor at the heart to an earthquake of soul-shattering inward revelation or amazed insight.

Poetry Expressing What Cannot be Put into Words

How does a poet use language to express what cannot be put into words? There is a useful exercise involving the names of emotions. The exercise asks people to list emotions, and opposite each emotion, to name an object which represents or condenses that emotion. This exercise relates the auditory and the visual in the way that a painter or sculptor might portray emotion.

Another exercise involves taking the emotions and opposite each one writing a situation or a story, expanding the previous exercise from object to action.

Discussion of Poetry

A good technique in discussion poetry is to have someone read a poem. Then ask if all in the group agree with the way it was read, and have the variants read. This allows the sound of the poem to sink in. Then take two steps:

(1) Paraphrase: put it into your own words. Can others agree on the paraphrase?
(2) How does the paraphrase differ from the poem?

With these steps, discussion and argument flow. Figures of speech and poetic devices disappear and reappear as the poem is put together again. Some may prefer the paraphrase; sometimes the poem is the paraphrase.

Further Tasks

Further work might examine figures of speech – simile and metaphor – dealing primarily with sense, and any poetic devices involved, with an emphasis on the ramification of sound as it relates to sense.

Other work might examine more deeply the musical effects in language itself in order to appreciate what potential for poetry (the creation of emotion and emotional experience) can lie in the realm of sound itself, or in music.

Still other work might examine more widely and deeply the connection between the senses and symbolism.

And still further work might evaluate examples representing both exceptions to what has been said, and transcendence beyond what has been considered.

The tasks never end.

EPILOGUE

On retirement, I spent two years making an anthology of poems for which I coined the word calliphony, from Greek kallos "beauty" and phone "sound" (like calligraphy – beautiful writing). Calliphony is a congruence between the sound of words and the sense of what is expressed. A printed page is silent as a musical score is silent; only when the writing is spoken does calliphony come to life. In the following example calliphony is found in a work of prose. Toward the end of Gone With the Wind, comes a short passage unlike writing in the rest of the novel;

> She thought of Tara, and it was as if a gentle cool hand were stealing over her heart. She could see the white house gleaming welcome to her through the reddening autumn leaves, feel the quiet hush of the country twilight coming down over her like a benediction, feel the dews falling on the acres of green bushes starred with fleecy white, see the raw color of the red earth and the dismal dark beauty of the pines on the rolling hills.

In this passage, I feel the meaning of Tara to Scarlett as nothing else in the book makes clear. I was told often how much Tara meant to her, but here I experience it. Everything rises to the simile "like a benediction", and ebbs away in vivid description. Tara is like her god! This is more poetry than it is prose.

Walking on the beach of the Land of Sense, the closer I wander to the high tide mark, the more sense predominates over sound; conversely, the closer I walk to the water's edge, the more sound predominates over sense. Wandering between the high and low water marks, I may encounter various styles and traditions of poetry.

Your response to what is heard may differ immensely from your response when you read silently. As an example, consider King Lear's curse on Goneril:

King Lear (1608): (I-iv:297-311)

Hear, nature hear;
Dear goddess hear! Suspend thy purpose, if
Thou didst intend to make this creature fruitful!
Into her womb convey sterility!
Dry up in her the organs of increase;
And from her derogate body never spring
A babe to honour her! If she must teem,
Create her child of spleen, that it may live
And be a thwart disnatur'd torment to her!
Let it stamp wrinkles in her brow of youth;
With cadent tears fret channels in her cheeks;
Turn all her mother's pains and benefits
To laughter and contempt, that she may feel
How sharper than a serpent's tooth it is
To have a thankless child!

Shakespeare (1564-1616)

The ugliness may be missed when you read the passage silently to yourself. But the ugliness can't be missed when you read it out loud to yourself. The disjunction of the words "thwart disnatur'd torment to her" and the lines following to the end emphasize that ugliness of sound. The sound itself is a curse.

In a last word, I would emphasize the personal aspect of response to any writing. Children lulled to sleep by a singing of the multiplication table may react life-long to it with comfort and pleasure as lullabies may evoke the same emotional response in other children. Personal experience is always unique.

I said before that language has very few words for emotions. In reading poetry, trust your body. It may stiffen with resolution, or shake with anger and hatred. Your eyes may stretch in wonder or awe. Your throat may close, or your eyes may fill with emotions like tenderness or sadness. Often you can't say exactly what you are feeling, but the visceral response clues you into an emotional experience that the language is creating. That emotional experience is poetry.

On the other hand, when you read a piece of writing called "poetry" to which you have no response at all, you may say that for you, this is not poetry. And it may turn out that you are speaking for many people. Trust your feelings.

Remember what I said of calliphony. A printed page is silent as a musical score is silent; only when the writing is spoken does calliphony come to life. Poetry is meant to be heard. Whenever the heart is moved by language, there you may find poetry.

The End